kraft foods

Busy Family
Recipes

Publications International, Ltd.

Pictured on the front cover: Cheesy Rice & Corn Casserole *(page 104)*.
Pictured on the back cover (clockwise from top): Baked Crab Rangoon *(page 20),* Shortcut Carrot Cake *(page 152),* and Taco Bake *(page 62).*

Microwave Cooking: Microwave ovens vary in wattage. Use the cooking times as guidelines and check for doneness before adding more time.

Preparation/Cooking Times: Preparation times are based on the approximate amount of time required to assemble the recipe before cooking, baking, chilling, or serving. These times include preparation steps such as measuring, chopping, and mixing. The fact that some preparations and cooking can be done simultaneously is taken into account. Preparation of optional ingredients and serving suggestions is not included.

8 7 6 5 4 3 2 1

contents

Welcome to Kraft Foods Busy Family Recipes,

your comprehensive solution to the daily dilemma of "what's for dinner?" Whether it's a quick after-school snack, a ready-in-seconds dip, a simple side dish, a no-bake dessert, or a crowd-pleasing casserole, we've got recipes and menus to suit every taste.

Need to entertain in a snap? Whip up tasty dips and small bites like Heavenly Ham Roll-Ups, VELVEETA Ultimate Queso Dip, or Last-Minute Cheesy Hot Dip. Potlucks and parties are made simple with dishes like 5-Minute Cheesy Broccoli Toss, STOVE TOP Easy Cheesy Chicken Bake, Shortcut Carrot Cake, and PHILADELPHIA 3-Step Key Lime Cheesecake. Looking to wow your family without spending a lot of time in the kitchen? We've got classic desserts like OREO Cookie Cream Pie, Angel Lush with Pineapple, and Turtle Pumpkin Pie, that will please everyone without a lot of cooking time or preparation. Even the kids will want to get involved in the fun, with creative microwaveable treats like NILLA Peppermint Cremes, Sweet Peanut Brittle, and Double-Dipped Strawberries.

We've collected more than 90 mouthwatering, family-pleasing favorites to enjoy year-round. So whether you're battling picky eaters or just a hectic schedule, Kraft Foods Busy Family Recipes has you covered with meal planning so easy, you'll never have to stress over dinner plans again.

Easy Appetizers & Snacks

Entertain in a snap

cheesy pizza dip

PREP: 10 min. | **TOTAL:** 15 min. | **MAKES:** 2½ cups or 20 servings, 2 Tbsp. each.

▶ what you need!

1 lb. (16 oz.) VELVEETA Pasteurized Prepared Cheese Product, cut into ½-inch cubes

1 tomato, chopped

20 pepperoni slices (1½ oz.), chopped

▶ make it!

1. **COMBINE** ingredients in 1½-qt. microwaveable bowl.

2. **MICROWAVE** on HIGH 4 to 5 min. or until VELVEETA is completely melted, stirring every 2 min.

3. **SERVE** hot with breadsticks or assorted cut-up fresh vegetables.

CREATIVE LEFTOVERS:
Refrigerate any leftover dip. Reheat and drizzle over hot baked potatoes or cooked pasta for an easy cheesy sauce.

favorite topped deviled eggs

PREP: 15 min. | TOTAL: 15 min. | MAKES: 24 servings.

▶ what you need!

12 hard-cooked eggs

4 oz. (½ of 8-oz. pkg.) PHILADELPHIA Neufchâtel Cheese, softened

3 Tbsp. KRAFT Light Mayo Reduced Fat Mayonnaise

2 tsp. GREY POUPON Dijon Mustard

2 tsp. white vinegar

1 tsp. sugar

⅛ tsp. paprika

▶ make it!

1. **CUT** eggs lengthwise in half. Remove yolks; place in medium bowl. Add all remaining ingredients except paprika; mix well.

2. **SPOON** into resealable plastic bag. Cut small corner from bottom of bag; pipe filling into egg whites. Sprinkle with paprika.

3. **ADD** Toppings, if desired.

TOPPING VARIATIONS:
Country Favorite: Top with 10 slices cooked and crumbled OSCAR MAYER Bacon and 2 finely chopped green onions. **It's Italian:** Top with ½ cup thinly sliced drained jarred sun-dried tomatoes packed in oil and ¼ cup thinly sliced fresh basil. **Fiesta Time:** Top with 6 Tbsp. finely chopped red peppers and 1 Tbsp. chopped cilantro. **Coastal Delight:** Top with ½ cup drained canned baby shrimp and 2 Tbsp. chopped fresh dill.

MAKE AHEAD:
Prepare as directed. Store in tightly covered container in refrigerator until ready to serve.

heavenly ham roll-ups

PREP: 15 min. | TOTAL: 35 min. | MAKES: 15 servings.

▶ what you need!

1 pkg. (9 oz.) OSCAR MAYER Deli Fresh Shaved Smoked Ham

5 Tbsp. PHILADELPHIA ⅓ Less Fat than Cream Cheese

15 fresh asparagus spears (about 1 lb.), trimmed

▶ make it!

HEAT oven to 350°F.

1. **FLATTEN** ham slices; pat dry. Stack in piles of 2 slices each; spread each stack with 1 tsp. reduced-fat cream cheese.

2. **PLACE** 1 asparagus spear on 1 long side of each ham stack; roll up. Place, seam-sides down, in 13×9-inch baking dish.

3. **BAKE** 15 to 20 min. or until heated through.

NO-BAKE HEAVENLY HAM ROLL-UPS:
Substitute frozen asparagus spears, cooked as directed on package, or canned asparagus spears, heated if desired, for the fresh asparagus. Assemble roll-ups as directed. Serve immediately. Or, cover and refrigerate until ready to serve.

FOOD FACTS:
Asparagus spears should be a bright green color and free of blemishes. Choose stalks that are straight, uniformly sized (either all thick or all thin) and firm. Stand fresh asparagus spears upright in a container filled with an inch of water. Cover with a plastic bag and refrigerate up to 3 days.

MAKE AHEAD:
Assemble roll-ups as directed. Refrigerate up to 24 hours before baking as directed.

SUBSTITUTE:
Prepare as directed, using 1 pkg. (6 oz.) OSCAR MAYER Thin Sliced Smoked Ham. Substitute 1 slice of ham for every 2 slices of the shaved ham.

flavor-infused cream cheese nibbles

PREP: 10 min. | TOTAL: 1 hour 10 min. | MAKES: 18 servings, 2 pieces each.

▶ what you need!

1 pkg. (8 oz.) PHILADELPHIA Cream Cheese

½ cup KRAFT Sun-Dried Tomato Dressing

2 cloves garlic, sliced

3 small sprigs fresh rosemary, stems removed

6 sprigs fresh thyme, chopped

1 tsp. black peppercorns

Peel of 1 lemon, cut into thin strips

▶ make it!

1. **CUT** cream cheese into 36 pieces; place in shallow dish.

2. **ADD** remaining ingredients; mix lightly.

3. **REFRIGERATE** 1 hour. Serve with NABISCO Crackers, crusty bread or pita chips.

CREATIVE LEFTOVERS:
Let the cheese come to room temperature before serving.

SHORTCUT:
To simplify, spread softened cream cheese onto bottom of 9-inch pie plate instead of cutting into pieces. Chop garlic, rosemary, thyme and lemon peel. Mix with dressing and ¼ tsp. ground black pepper; spread over cream cheese. Serve as directed.

MAKE AHEAD:
Appetizer can be stored in refrigerator up to 24 hours before serving.

PHILLY shrimp cocktail dip

▸ what you need!

1 pkg. (8 oz.) PHILADELPHIA Cream Cheese, softened

¾ lb. cooked cleaned shrimp, chopped (about 2 cups)

¾ cup KRAFT Cocktail Sauce

¼ cup KRAFT Shredded Parmesan Cheese

2 green onions, sliced

▸ make it!

1. **SPREAD** cream cheese onto bottom of shallow bowl.

2. **TOSS** shrimp with cocktail sauce; spoon over cream cheese.

3. **TOP** with remaining ingredients. Serve with WHEAT THINS Original Crackers.

SUBSTITUTE:
Substitute 1 pkg. (8 oz.) imitation crabmeat, coarsely chopped, for the shrimp.

PHILLY mediterranean dip

PREP: 10 min. | TOTAL: 10 min. | MAKES: 1½ cups or 12 servings, 2 Tbsp. each.

▸ what you need!

1 pkg. (8 oz.) PHILADELPHIA Neufchâtel Cheese, softened

½ cup chopped seedless cucumbers

1 plum tomato, chopped

2 Tbsp. finely chopped red onions

2 Tbsp. KRAFT Greek Vinaigrette Dressing

▸ make it!

1. **SPREAD** Neufchâtel onto bottom of 9-inch pie plate.

2. **COMBINE** remaining ingredients; spoon over Neufchâtel.

3. **SERVE** with WHEAT THINS Original Crackers or assorted cut-up fresh vegetables.

HOW TO SOFTEN NEUFCHÂTEL CHEESE:
Place completely unwrapped Neufchâtel in microwaveable 9-inch pie plate. Microwave on HIGH 15 sec. or just until softened. Spread onto bottom of pie plate, then continue as directed.

cream cheese-bacon crescents

PREP: 15 min. | TOTAL: 30 min. | MAKES: 16 servings.

▶ what you need!

1 tub (8 oz.) PHILADELPHIA Chive & Onion Cream Cheese Spread

3 slices OSCAR MAYER Bacon, cooked, crumbled

2 cans (8 oz. each) refrigerated crescent dinner rolls

▶ make it!

HEAT oven to 375°F.

1. **MIX** cream cheese spread and bacon until well blended.

2. **SEPARATE** each can of dough into 8 triangles. Cut each triangle lengthwise in half. Spread each dough triangle with 1 generous tsp. cream cheese mixture. Roll up, starting at shortest side of triangle; place, point sides down, on baking sheet.

3. **BAKE** 12 to 15 min. or until golden brown. Serve warm.

HEALTHY LIVING:
For a reduced-fat version, prepare using PHILADELPHIA Chive & Onion Light Cream Cheese Spread and reduced-fat refrigerated crescent dinner rolls. As a bonus, these changes will save 30 calories per serving.

VARIATION:
For a sweet version, prepare using PHILADELPHIA Strawberry Cream Cheese Spread and substituting chopped PLANTERS Walnuts for the bacon.

baked crab rangoon

PREP: 20 min. | TOTAL: 40 min. | MAKES: 12 servings.

▶ what you need!

4 oz. (½ of 8-oz. pkg.) PHILADELPHIA Neufchâtel Cheese, softened

1 can (6 oz.) crabmeat, drained, flaked

2 green onions, thinly sliced

¼ cup KRAFT Light Mayo Reduced Fat Mayonnaise

12 wonton wrappers

▶ make it!

HEAT oven to 350°F.

1. **MIX** first 4 ingredients.

2. **PLACE** 1 wonton wrapper in each of 12 muffin cups sprayed with cooking spray, extending edges of wrappers over sides of cups. Fill with crab mixture.

3. **BAKE** 18 to 20 min. or until edges of cups are golden brown and filling is heated through.

SPECIAL EXTRA:
Garnish with additional green onions, cut into strips, just before serving.

savory parmesan bites

▶ what you need!

1 pkg. (8 oz.) PHILADELPHIA Cream Cheese, softened

1 cup KRAFT Grated Parmesan Cheese, divided

2 cans (8 oz. each) refrigerated crescent dinner rolls

1 red pepper, chopped

¼ cup chopped fresh parsley

▶ make it!

HEAT oven to 350°F.

1. **BEAT** cream cheese and ¾ cup Parmesan with mixer until well blended.

2. **SEPARATE** dough into 8 rectangles; seal seams. Spread with cream cheese mixture; top with peppers and parsley. Fold each rectangle lengthwise into thirds to enclose filling; cut each into 4 squares. Place, seam-sides down, on baking sheet; top with remaining Parmesan.

3. **BAKE** 13 to 15 min. or until golden brown.

SIZE-WISE:
At your next party, select a few of your favorite appetizers rather than sampling one of each to save room for your entrée.

VARIATION:
Substitute 1 jar (13¼ oz.) sliced mushrooms or 1 pkg. (3 oz.) pepperoni slices for the red peppers and parsley.

five-layer italian dip

PREP: 10 min. | TOTAL: 25 min. | MAKES: 2 cups or 16 servings, 2 Tbsp. each.

▸ what you need!

1 pkg. (8 oz.) PHILADELPHIA Cream Cheese, softened

¼ cup KRAFT Grated Parmesan Cheese

⅓ cup pesto

½ cup roasted red peppers, drained, chopped

1 cup KRAFT Shredded Mozzarella Cheese

▸ make it!

HEAT oven to 350°F.

1. **MIX** cream cheese and Parmesan; spread onto bottom of 9-inch pie plate.

2. **LAYER** remaining ingredients over cream cheese mixture.

3. **BAKE** 15 min. or until heated through. Serve with assorted NABISCO Crackers or sliced Italian bread.

VARIATION:
Prepare using PHILADELPHIA Neufchâtel Cheese and KRAFT 2% Milk Shredded Mozzarella Cheese.

SPECIAL EXTRA:
Garnish with sliced black olives and fresh basil leaves just before serving.

VELVEETA ultimate queso dip

PREP: 5 min. | TOTAL: 10 min. | MAKES: 3 cups or 24 servings, 2 Tbsp. each.

▶ what you need!

1 lb. (16 oz.) VELVEETA
Pasteurized Prepared
Cheese Product, cut into
½-inch cubes

1 can (10 oz.)
RO*TEL Diced Tomatoes &
Green Chilies, undrained

▶ make it!

1. **MIX** ingredients in microwaveable bowl.

2. **MICROWAVE** on HIGH 5 min. or until VELVEETA is completely melted, stirring after 3 min.

3. **SERVE** with assorted cut-up fresh vegetables, WHEAT THINS Crackers or tortilla chips.

SIZE-WISE:
When eating appetizers at a social occasion, preview your choices and decide which you'd like to try instead of taking some of each.

Ro*Tel is a product of ConAgra Foods, Inc.

cheesy spinach and bacon dip

PREP: 10 min. | TOTAL: 15 min. | MAKES: 4 cups or 32 servings, 2 Tbsp. each.

▸ what you need!

- 1 pkg. (10 oz.) frozen chopped spinach, thawed, drained

- 1 lb. (16 oz.) VELVEETA Pasteurized Prepared Cheese Product, cut into ½-inch cubes

- 4 oz. (½ of 8-oz. pkg.) PHILADELPHIA Cream Cheese, cubed

- 1 can (10 oz.) RO*TEL Diced Tomatoes & Green Chilies, undrained

- 8 slices OSCAR MAYER Bacon, cooked, crumbled

▸ make it!

1. **MICROWAVE** all ingredients in microwaveable bowl on HIGH 5 min. or until VELVEETA is completely melted and mixture is well blended, stirring after 3 min.

2. **SERVE** with tortilla chips and cut-up fresh vegetables.

USE YOUR SLOW COOKER:
When serving this dip at a party, pour the prepared dip into a small slow cooker set on LOW. This will keep the dip warm and at the ideal consistency for several hours. For best results, stir the dip occasionally to prevent hot spots.

Ro*Tel is a product of ConAgra Foods, Inc.

hot broccoli dip

PREP: 30 min. | TOTAL: 30 min. | MAKES: 2½ cups or 20 servings, 2 Tbsp. each.

▶ what you need!

1 loaf (1½ lb.) round sourdough bread

½ cup chopped celery

½ cup chopped red peppers

¼ cup chopped onions

2 Tbsp. butter or margarine

1 lb. (16 oz.) VELVEETA Pasteurized Prepared Cheese Product, cut into ½-inch cubes

1 pkg. (10 oz.) frozen chopped broccoli, thawed, drained

¼ tsp. dried rosemary leaves, crushed

Few drops hot pepper sauce

▶ make it!

HEAT oven to 350°F.

1. **CUT** slice from top of bread loaf; remove center, leaving 1-inch-thick shell. Cut removed bread into bite-size pieces. Cover shell with top of bread; place on baking sheet with bread pieces. Bake 15 min. Cool slightly.

2. **MEANWHILE,** cook and stir celery, red peppers and onions in butter in medium saucepan on medium heat until tender. Add VELVEETA; cook on low heat until melted, stirring frequently. Add broccoli, rosemary and hot pepper sauce; cook until heated through, stirring constantly.

3. **SPOON** into bread loaf. Serve with toasted bread pieces, NABISCO Crackers and/or assorted cut-up fresh vegetables.

VELVEETA spicy cheeseburger dip

PREP: 5 min. | TOTAL: 10 min. | MAKES: 4½ cups or 36 servings, 2 Tbsp. each.

▶ what you need!

1 lb. (16 oz.) VELVEETA Pasteurized Prepared Cheese Product, cut into ½-inch cubes

1 can (10 oz.) RO*TEL Diced Tomatoes & Green Chilies, undrained

1 cup KRAFT Shredded Low-Moisture Part-Skim Mozzarella Cheese

½ lb. ground beef, cooked, drained

4 green onions, sliced

▶ make it!

1. **MIX** all ingredients except onions in microwaveable bowl.

2. **MICROWAVE** on HIGH 5 min. or until VELVEETA is melted, stirring after 3 min. Stir in onions.

3. **SERVE** with RITZ Crackers and assorted cut-up fresh vegetables.

Ro*Tel is a product of ConAgra Foods, Inc.

USE YOUR STOVE:
Mix all ingredients except onions in medium saucepan; cook on medium heat 5 to 7 min. or until VELVEETA is melted, stirring frequently. Stir in onions. Serve as directed.

last-minute cheesy hot dip

PREP: 10 min. | TOTAL: 25 min. | MAKES: 2½ cups or 20 servings, 2 Tbsp. dip and 4 crackers each.

▶ what you need!

1 pkg. (8 oz.) PHILADELPHIA Cream Cheese, softened

1½ cups KRAFT Shredded Colby & Monterey Jack Cheese

5 green onions, thinly sliced

⅓ cup KRAFT Mayo Real Mayonnaise

1 Tbsp. GREY POUPON Harvest Coarse Ground Mustard

2 Tbsp. chopped PLANTERS Smoked Almonds

RITZ Simply Socials Golden Wheat Crackers

▶ make it!

HEAT oven to 350°F.

1. **MIX** cheeses, onions, mayo and mustard in 9-inch pie plate; top with almonds.

2. **BAKE** 15 min. Serve with crackers.

SERVING SUGGESTION:
Serve with WHEAT THINS Toasted Chips Multi-Grain.

WHEAT THINS
salmon snackers

PREP: 5 min. | TOTAL: 5 min. | MAKES: 3 servings, 2 topped crackers each.

▸ what you need!

6 WHEAT THINS Big Snack Crackers

2 Tbsp. PHILADELPHIA Light Cream Cheese Spread

1½ oz. smoked salmon, cut into 6 pieces

6 sprigs fresh dill

▸ make it!

1. **SPREAD** crackers with cream cheese spread.

2. **TOP** with salmon and dill.

SUBSTITUTE:
Substitute chopped fresh chives for the dill.

SPECIAL EXTRA:
Garnish with lemon zest or small strips of lemon peel.

chinatown chicken wings

▸ what you need!

¾ cup KRAFT GOOD SEASONS Asian Sesame with Ginger Dressing

¼ cup KRAFT THICK 'N SPICY Brown Sugar Barbecue Sauce

12 chicken wings (2 lb.), split, tips removed

1 cup PLANTERS Dry Roasted Peanuts, finely chopped

12 RITZ Crackers, crushed

▸ make it!

HEAT oven to 400°F.

1. **MIX** dressing and barbecue sauce in large bowl. Remove ½ cup of the dressing mixture for later use. Add chicken to remaining dressing mixture; toss to coat.

2. **MIX** nuts and cracker crumbs. Add wing pieces, 1 at a time; turn to evenly coat chicken. Place in single layer on baking sheet.

3. **BAKE** 20 to 25 min. or until wings are lightly browned and cooked through. Serve as dippers with the reserved dressing mixture.

SUBSTITUTE:
Substitute 1 lb. boneless skinless chicken breasts, cut into 1-inch pieces, for the wing pieces.

chicken divan toppers

▶ what you need!

2 oz. (⅓ of 6-oz. pkg.) KRAFT Natural 2% Milk Blend of Reduced Fat Monterey Jack, Mild Cheddar & Colby Cheeses, cut into 8 slices

1 cooked small boneless skinless chicken breast half (¼ lb.), cut into 16 slices

2 Tbsp. BREAKSTONE'S Reduced Fat or KNUDSEN Light Sour Cream

1 tsp. GREY POUPON Harvest Coarse Ground Mustard

16 TRISCUIT Rosemary & Olive Oil Crackers

16 small broccoli florets, cooked

▶ make it!

HEAT oven to 350°F.

1. **CUT** cheese slices diagonally in half. Toss chicken with sour cream and mustard.

2. **PLACE** crackers on baking sheet. Top with chicken, cheese and broccoli.

3. **BAKE** 8 to 10 min. or until cheese is melted.

SPECIAL EXTRA:
Sprinkle lightly with cracked black pepper or paprika before baking.

SUBSTITUTE:
Substitute KRAFT Mayo with Olive Oil Reduced Fat Mayonnaise for the sour cream.

fire-roasted avocado toppers

▶ what you need!

¼ cup KRAFT Reduced Fat Mayonnaise with Olive Oil

1 avocado, chopped

4 cherry tomatoes, chopped

1 Tbsp. finely chopped cilantro

1 Tbsp. fresh lime juice

48 TRISCUIT Fire Roasted Tomato & Olive Oil Crackers

▶ make it!

1. **COMBINE** all ingredients except crackers.

2. **SPREAD** onto crackers.

SPECIAL EXTRA:
Garnish with additional cilantro just before serving.

cheesy spinach and artichoke dip

PREP: 10 min. | TOTAL: 30 min. | MAKES: 2¾ cups or 22 servings, 2 Tbsp. each.

▶ what you need!

1 can (14 oz.) artichoke hearts, drained, finely chopped

1 pkg. (10 oz.) frozen chopped spinach, thawed, drained

¾ cup KRAFT Grated Parmesan Cheese

¾ cup KRAFT Light Mayo Reduced Fat Mayonnaise

½ cup KRAFT 2% Milk Shredded Mozzarella Cheese

½ tsp. garlic powder

▶ make it!

HEAT oven to 350°F.

1. **MIX** all ingredients; spoon into 9-inch quiche dish or pie plate.

2. **BAKE** 20 min. or until heated through.

3. **SERVE** with TRISCUIT Reduced Fat Crackers and assorted cut-up fresh vegetables.

SPECIAL EXTRA:
Substitute 1 env. (0.7 oz.) GOOD SEASONS Italian Salad Dressing Mix for the garlic powder.

AWESOME SPINACH AND MUSHROOM DIP:
Substitute 1 cup chopped mushrooms for the artichokes.

Casseroles & Entrées

Hearty family favorites

quick pasta carbonara

PREP: 20 min. | TOTAL: 20 min. | MAKES: 4 servings, 1¼ cups each.

▶ what you need!

½ lb. fettuccine, uncooked

4 slices OSCAR MAYER Bacon, chopped

4 oz. (½ of 8-oz. pkg.) PHILADELPHIA Cream Cheese, cubed

1 cup frozen peas

¾ cup milk

½ cup KRAFT Grated Parmesan Cheese

½ tsp. garlic powder

▶ make it!

1. **COOK** fettuccine as directed on package. Meanwhile, cook bacon in large skillet until crisp. Remove bacon from skillet with slotted spoon, reserving 2 Tbsp. drippings in skillet. Drain bacon on paper towels.

2. **ADD** remaining ingredients to reserved drippings; cook on low heat until cream cheese is melted and mixture is well blended and heated through.

3. **DRAIN** fettuccine; place in large bowl. Add cream cheese sauce and bacon; mix lightly.

KEEPING IT SAFE:
When a dish contains dairy products, such as the cheeses and milk in this recipe, be sure to serve it immediately and refrigerate any leftovers promptly.

SUBSTITUTE:
Prepare using PHILADELPHIA Neufchâtel Cheese.

spaghetti a la PHILLY

PREP: 25 min. | TOTAL: 25 min. | MAKES: 6 servings.

▶ what you need!

¾ lb. spaghetti, uncooked

1 lb. lean ground beef

1 jar (24 oz.) spaghetti sauce

4 oz. (½ of 8-oz. pkg.) PHILADELPHIA Cream Cheese, cubed

2 Tbsp. KRAFT Grated Parmesan Cheese

▶ make it!

1. **COOK** spaghetti as directed on package.

2. **MEANWHILE,** brown meat in large skillet; drain. Return meat to skillet. Stir in sauce and cream cheese; cook on low heat 3 to 5 min. or until sauce is well blended and heated through, stirring frequently.

3. **DRAIN** spaghetti. Add to sauce; mix lightly. Place on platter; top with Parmesan.

SPECIAL EXTRA:
Cook 1 cup each chopped green peppers and onions with the ground beef.

SUBSTITUTE:
Prepare using ground turkey and PHILADELPHIA Neufchâtel Cheese.

easy shepherd's pie

▸ what you need!

1 lb. ground beef

2 cups hot mashed potatoes

4 oz. (½ of 8-oz. pkg.) PHILADELPHIA Cream Cheese, cubed

1 cup KRAFT Shredded Cheddar Cheese, divided

2 cloves garlic, minced

4 cups frozen mixed vegetables, thawed

1 cup beef gravy

▸ make it!

HEAT oven to 375°F.

1. **BROWN** meat in large skillet; drain.

2. **MEANWHILE,** mix potatoes, cream cheese, ½ cup Cheddar and garlic until well blended.

3. **ADD** vegetables and gravy to meat; mix well. Spoon into 9-inch square baking dish.

4. **COVER** with potato mixture and remaining Cheddar. Bake 20 min. or until heated through.

HEALTHY LIVING:
Save 70 calories and 9 grams of fat, including 5 grams of saturated fat, per serving by preparing with extra-lean ground beef, PHILADELPHIA Neufchâtel Cheese and KRAFT 2% Milk Shredded Cheddar Cheese.

BARBECUE SHEPHERD'S PIE:
Prepare omitting the garlic and substituting ¾ cup KRAFT Original Barbecue Sauce mixed with ½ tsp. onion powder for the gravy.

CREATIVE LEFTOVERS:
This recipe is a great way to use leftover mashed potatoes.

20-minute skillet salmon

PREP: 10 min. | TOTAL: 20 min. | MAKES: 4 servings.

▶ what you need!

1 Tbsp. oil

4 salmon fillets (1 lb.)

1 cup fat-free milk

½ cup (½ of 8-oz. tub) PHILADELPHIA ⅓ Less Fat than Cream Cheese

½ cup chopped cucumbers

2 Tbsp. chopped fresh dill

▶ make it!

1. HEAT oil in large skillet on medium-high heat. Add fish; cook 5 min. on each side or until fish flakes easily with fork. Remove from skillet; cover to keep warm.

2. ADD milk and reduced-fat cream cheese to skillet; cook and stir until cream cheese is completely melted and mixture is well blended. Stir in cucumbers and dill.

3. RETURN fish to skillet. Cook 2 min. or until heated through. Serve topped with cream cheese sauce.

SERVING SUGGESTION:
Round out the meal with hot cooked rice and steamed vegetables. Or serve salmon on a bed of salad greens.

COOKING KNOW-HOW:
When salmon is done, it will appear opaque and flake easily with fork.

FOOD FACTS:
Check salmon fillets for bones before cooking by running fingers over surface. Small bumps are usually a sign of bones—use tweezers to remove them.

creamy chicken and pasta casserole

PREP: 15 min. | TOTAL: 40 min. | MAKES: 6 servings.

▸ what you need!

¾ cup each: chopped celery, red onions and red peppers

1 pkg. (8 oz.) PHILADELPHIA Cream Cheese, cubed

2 cups milk

¼ tsp. garlic salt

4 cups cooked rotini pasta

3 cups chopped cooked chicken breasts

½ cup KRAFT 100% Grated Parmesan Cheese, divided

▸ make it!

HEAT oven to 350°F.

1. **HEAT** large nonstick skillet sprayed with cooking spray on medium heat. Add vegetables; cook and stir 3 min. or until crisp-tender. Add cream cheese, milk and garlic salt; cook on low heat 3 to 5 min. or until cream cheese is melted, stirring frequently.

2. **ADD** pasta, chicken and ¼ cup Parmesan cheese; spoon into 2½-qt. casserole dish.

3. **BAKE** 20 to 25 min. or until heated through. Sprinkle with remaining Parmesan cheese.

SERVING SUGGESTION:
Serve with a mixed green salad tossed with your favorite KRAFT Dressing.

VARIATION:
Prepare using PHILADELPHIA Neufchâtel Cheese, ⅓ Less Fat than Cream Cheese; skim milk and whole wheat rotini pasta.

easy parmesan-garlic chicken

PREP: 5 min. | TOTAL: 30 min. | MAKES: 6 servings.

▶ what you need!

½ cup KRAFT Grated Parmesan Cheese

1 env. (0.7 oz.) GOOD SEASONS Italian Dressing Mix

½ tsp. garlic powder

6 boneless skinless chicken breast halves (2 lb.)

▶ make it!

HEAT oven to 400°F.

1. **MIX** cheese, dressing mix and garlic powder.

2. **MOISTEN** chicken with water; coat with cheese mixture. Place in shallow baking dish.

3. **BAKE** 20 to 25 min. or until chicken is done (165°F).

SPECIAL EXTRA:
For a golden appearance, after chicken is cooked through set oven to Broil. Place 6 inches from heat. Broil 2 to 4 min. or until chicken is golden brown.

VARIATIONS:
Prepare as directed, choosing one of the following flavor combinations:
Mediterranean Parmesan Chicken: Substitute 1 Tbsp. lemon zest and 1 tsp. dried oregano leaves for the garlic powder.
Parmesan-Onion Chicken: Substitute 2 Tbsp. minced onion flakes for the garlic powder.
Spicy Parmesan Chicken: Substitute ground red pepper (cayenne) for the garlic powder.
Parmesan Pizza Chicken: Substitute 1 tsp. dried basil leaves and ¼ tsp. crushed red pepper for the garlic powder.

KEEPING IT SAFE:
Place frozen chicken under cold running water to thaw. Be sure to use cold water and keep the chicken in its original wrap or place in water-tight resealable plastic bag while thawing it. Also, be careful not to cross-contaminate other food products, work surfaces or utensils with the dripping water.

easy italian pasta bake

PREP: 20 min. | TOTAL: 40 min. | MAKES: 6 servings, 1⅓ cups each.

▶ what you need!

1 lb. extra-lean ground beef

3 cups whole wheat penne pasta, cooked, drained

1 jar (26 oz.) spaghetti sauce

⅓ cup KRAFT Grated Parmesan Cheese, divided

1½ cups KRAFT 2% Milk Shredded Mozzarella Cheese

▶ make it!

HEAT oven to 375°F.

1. **BROWN** meat in large skillet; drain. Add pasta, sauce and ½ the Parmesan; mix well.

2. **SPOON** into 13×9-inch dish; top with remaining cheeses.

3. **BAKE** 20 min. or until heated through.

SUBSTITUTE:
Prepare using regular penne pasta.

VARIATION:
Substitute 2 cups BOCA Ground Crumbles for the ground beef. No need to brown or thaw the crumbles in skillet—simply combine with the pasta, sauce and Parmesan cheese; spoon into baking dish and bake as directed.

SPECIAL EXTRA:
Brown meat with 1 tsp. Italian seasoning and 3 cloves garlic, minced.

turkey-parmesan casserole

PREP: 20 min. | TOTAL: 50 min. | MAKES: 6 servings, 1⅓ cups each.

▶ what you need!

8 oz. spaghetti, broken in half, uncooked

1 can (10¾ oz.) condensed cream of mushroom soup

¾ cup BREAKSTONE'S or KNUDSEN Sour Cream

¼ cup milk

⅓ cup KRAFT Grated Parmesan Cheese

¼ tsp. black pepper

3 cups frozen broccoli florets, thawed

2 cups chopped cooked turkey

▶ make it!

HEAT oven to 350°F.

1. **COOK** spaghetti as directed on package; drain.

2. **MIX** soup, sour cream, milk, Parmesan cheese and pepper in large bowl. Add spaghetti, broccoli and turkey; mix lightly. Spoon into 2-quart casserole.

3. **BAKE** 25 to 30 minutes or until heated through.

SERVING SUGGESTION:
Serve with a crisp, mixed green salad, a whole wheat roll and fresh fruit for dessert.

taco bake

PREP: 15 min. | TOTAL: 35 min. | MAKES: 6 servings, 1 cup each.

▶ what you need!

1 pkg. (14 oz.) KRAFT Deluxe Macaroni & Cheese Dinner

1 lb. ground beef

1 pkg. (1¼ oz.) TACO BELL® HOME ORIGINALS® Taco Seasoning Mix

¾ cup BREAKSTONE'S or KNUDSEN Sour Cream

1½ cups KRAFT Shredded Cheddar Cheese, divided

1 cup TACO BELL® HOME ORIGINALS® Thick 'N Chunky Salsa

▶ make it!

HEAT oven to 400°F.

1. **PREPARE** Dinner as directed on package. While Macaroni is cooking, cook meat with taco seasoning as directed on package.

2. **STIR** sour cream into prepared Dinner; spoon ½ into 8-inch square baking dish. Top with layers of meat mixture, 1 cup cheese and remaining Dinner mixture; cover with foil.

3. **BAKE** 15 min.; top with salsa and remaining cheese. Bake, uncovered, 5 min. or until cheese is melted.

TACO BELL® and HOME ORIGINALS® are trademarks owned and licensed by Taco Bell Corp.

SIZE-WISE:
Keep an eye on portion size when you enjoy this hearty meal.

SPECIAL EXTRA:
For extra crunch, prepare and bake as directed, topping with ½ cup coarsely crushed tortilla chips along with the salsa and cheese.

cheesy tuna noodle casserole

PREP: 10 min. | TOTAL: 49 min. | MAKES: 5 servings, about 1½ cups each.

▶ what you need!

1 pkg. (16 oz.) frozen vegetable blend (broccoli, carrots, cauliflower)

1 pkg. (14 oz.) KRAFT Deluxe Macaroni & Cheese Dinner Made With 2% Milk Cheese

¾ cup fat-free milk

¼ cup KRAFT Light Zesty Italian Dressing

1 can (12 oz.) white tuna in water, drained

1 cup KRAFT 2% Milk Shredded Sharp Cheddar Cheese, divided

▶ make it!

HEAT oven to 375°F.

1. **PLACE** vegetables in colander in sink. Cook Macaroni as directed on package; pour over vegetables to drain macaroni and thaw vegetables. Return to saucepan.

2. **STIR** in Cheese Sauce, milk and dressing. Add tuna and ½ cup Cheddar; mix well. Spoon into 2-qt. casserole; cover.

3. **BAKE** 35 min. or until heated through. Top with remaining Cheddar; bake 3 to 4 min. or until melted.

SUBSTITUTE:
Substitute 1 lb. extra-lean ground beef, cooked and drained, for the tuna.

MAKE AHEAD:
Assemble casserole as directed. Refrigerate up to 24 hours. When ready to serve, bake, covered, at 375°F for 40 to 45 min. or until heated through. Top with remaining cheese; continue as directed.

SUBSTITUTE:
Prepare using 2 (5 oz. each) cans tuna.

layered enchilada bake

PREP: 15 min. | TOTAL: 1 hour 10 min. | MAKES: 8 servings.

▸ what you need!

1 lb. lean ground beef

1 large onion, chopped

2 cups TACO BELL® HOME ORIGINALS® Thick 'N Chunky Salsa

1 can (15 oz.) black beans, drained, rinsed

¼ cup KRAFT Zesty Italian Dressing

2 Tbsp. TACO BELL® HOME ORIGINALS® Taco Seasoning Mix

6 flour tortillas (8 inch)

1 cup BREAKSTONE'S or KNUDSEN Sour Cream

1 pkg. (8 oz.) KRAFT Mexican Style Finely Shredded Four Cheese

▸ make it!

HEAT oven to 400°F.

1. **BROWN** meat with onions in large skillet on medium-high heat; drain. Stir in salsa, beans, dressing and seasoning mix.

2. **ARRANGE** 3 tortillas on bottom of 13×9-inch baking dish; cover with layers of half each meat mixture, sour cream and cheese. Repeat layers. Cover with foil.

3. **BAKE** 40 min. or until casserole is heated through and cheese is melted, removing foil after 30 min. Let stand 5 min. before cutting to serve.

TACO BELL® and HOME ORIGINALS® are trademarks owned and licensed by Taco Bell Corp.

VELVEETA cheesy pasta casserole

PREP: 15 min. | TOTAL: 55 min. | MAKES: 8 servings, 1½ cups each.

▶ what you need!

1½ lb. boneless skinless chicken breasts, cut into bite-size pieces

4 cups cooked rotini pasta

1 pkg. (1 lb.) frozen Italian-style vegetable combination, thawed, drained

1 can (10 oz.) RO*TEL Diced Tomatoes & Green Chilies, undrained

¾ lb. (12 oz.) VELVEETA Pasteurized Prepared Cheese Product, cut into ½-inch cubes

▶ make it!

HEAT oven to 400°F.

1. **COMBINE** ingredients in 13×9-inch baking dish; cover.

2. **BAKE** 40 min. Let stand 5 min.; stir until sauce is well blended.

Ro*Tel is a product of ConAgra Foods, Inc.

SHORTCUT:
Have leftover chicken? Prepare recipe as directed, using 5 cups chopped cooked chicken and reducing the baking time to 20 to 25 min. or until VELVEETA is melted and casserole is heated through.

SUBSTITUTE:
For milder flavor, prepare using 14½-oz. can plain diced tomatoes.

better-than-ever cheesy meat lasagna

PREP: 30 min. | TOTAL: 1 hour 5 min. | MAKES: 9 servings.

▸ what you need!

¾ lb. extra-lean ground beef

3 cloves garlic, minced

1½ tsp. dried oregano leaves

1 jar (26 oz.) spaghetti sauce

1 large tomato, chopped

1 egg

1 container (16 oz.) BREAKSTONE'S or KNUDSEN 2% Milkfat Low Fat Cottage Cheese

¼ cup KRAFT Grated Parmesan Cheese

9 lasagna noodles, cooked, drained

1 pkg. (7 oz.) KRAFT 2% Milk Shredded Mozzarella Cheese, divided

▸ make it!

HEAT oven to 375°F.

1. **BROWN** meat with garlic and oregano in large saucepan. Stir in spaghetti sauce; simmer 5 min., stirring occasionally. Remove from heat; stir in tomatoes.

2. **MIX** egg, cottage cheese and Parmesan. Spread ½ cup spaghetti sauce mixture onto bottom of 13×9-inch baking dish. Top with layers of 3 noodles, 1 cup cottage cheese mixture, ½ cup mozzarella and 1 cup remaining sauce. Repeat layers. Top with remaining noodles and sauce; cover.

3. BAKE 30 min. or until heated through. Uncover; top with remaining mozzarella. Bake, uncovered, 5 min. or until mozzarella is melted. Let stand 5 min. before serving.

VARIATION:
Substitute 2 pouches (2 cups) frozen BOCA Ground Crumbles for the browned ground beef. Add to spaghetti sauce in saucepan along with the garlic and oregano; cook until heated through, stirring occasionally. Continue as directed.

MAKEOVER - HOW WE DID IT:
We've made over a traditional lasagna that results in a savings of 120 calories and 10 grams of fat, including 6.5 grams of saturated fat, per serving. We replaced the sausage with extra-lean ground beef and decreased the amount, used cottage cheese in place of ricotta cheese, decreased the Parmesan and used KRAFT 2% Milk Shredded Mozzarella Cheese.

MAKE AHEAD:
Assemble lasagna as directed. Refrigerate up to 24 hours. When ready to serve, bake, covered, at 375°F for 40 min. or until heated through.

STOVE TOP
easy cheesy chicken bake

PREP: 10 min. | TOTAL: 40 min. | MAKES: 6 servings.

▶ what you need!

1 pkg. (6 oz.) STOVE TOP Stuffing Mix for Chicken

1½ lb. boneless skinless chicken breasts, cut into bite-size pieces

1 pkg. (14 oz.) frozen broccoli florets, thawed, drained

1 can (10¾ oz.) condensed cream of chicken soup

½ cup milk

1½ cups KRAFT Shredded Cheddar Cheese

▶ make it!

HEAT oven to 400°F.

1. **PREPARE** stuffing as directed on package.

2. **COMBINE** chicken and broccoli in 13×9-inch baking dish. Stir in soup, milk and cheese; top with stuffing.

3. **BAKE** 30 min. or until chicken is done and casserole is heated through.

SUBSTITUTE:
Prepare using fresh broccoli florets.

bruschetta chicken bake

PREP: 10 min. | TOTAL: 40 min. | MAKES: 6 servings.

▶ what you need!

1 can (14½ oz.) diced tomatoes, undrained

1 pkg. (6 oz.) STOVE TOP Stuffing Mix for Chicken

½ cup water

2 cloves garlic, minced

1½ lb. boneless skinless chicken breasts, cut into bite-size pieces

1 tsp. dried basil leaves

1 cup KRAFT 2% Milk Shredded Mozzarella Cheese

▶ make it!

HEAT oven to 400°F.

1. **MIX** tomatoes, stuffing mix, water and garlic just until stuffing mix is moistened.

2. **LAYER** chicken, basil and cheese in 3-qt. casserole or 13×9-inch baking dish.

3. **TOP** with stuffing. Bake 30 min. or until chicken is done.

MAKE AHEAD:
Prepare and bake as directed; cool. Refrigerate up to 24 hours. To reheat, spoon each serving onto microwaveable plate. Microwave on HIGH 2 to 3 min. or until heated through.

NUTRITION BONUS:
Make this flavorful chicken recipe tonight as part of an easy weeknight dinner. As a bonus, the cheese is a good source of calcium. For complete nutritional information, please visit www.kraftfoods.com.

layered meatball bake

PREP: 10 min. | TOTAL: 35 min. | MAKES: 6 servings.

▶ what you need!

1 pkg. (6 oz.) STOVE TOP Stuffing Mix for Chicken

1 can (10¾ oz.) reduced-sodium condensed cream of mushroom soup

¼ cup milk

1 pkg. (1 lb.) frozen meatballs

2 cups frozen peas

1 cup KRAFT 2% Milk Shredded Cheddar Cheese

▶ make it!

HEAT oven to 400°F.

1. **PREPARE** stuffing as directed on package.

2. **MIX** soup and milk in 13×9-inch baking dish. Stir in meatballs and peas; sprinkle with cheese. Top with stuffing.

3. **BAKE** 20 to 25 min. or until heated through.

SERVING SUGGESTION:
Serve this main dish with a mixed green salad for a quick and tasty weekday meal.

VARIATION:
Prepare as directed, substituting 1 can (14½ oz.) diced tomatoes for the soup, omitting milk and using Italian-flavored meatballs and KRAFT Shredded Low-Moisture Part-Skim Mozzarella Cheese.

chili-beef stuffing bake

PREP: 10 min. | TOTAL: 40 min. | MAKES: 6 servings.

▶ what you need!

1½ cups hot water

1 pkg. (6 oz.) STOVE TOP Cornbread Stuffing Mix

1½ lb. lean ground beef

1 can (15 oz.) kidney beans, undrained

1 can (8 oz.) tomato sauce

1 cup TACO BELL® HOME ORIGINALS® Thick 'N Chunky Salsa

1 cup KRAFT Shredded Cheddar Cheese

▶ make it!

HEAT oven to 400°F.

1. **ADD** hot water to stuffing mix; stir just until moistened.

2. **BROWN** meat in large skillet; drain. Stir in beans, tomato sauce and salsa. Spoon into 2-qt. casserole; top with cheese and stuffing.

3. **BAKE** 30 min. or until heated through.

SUBSTITUTE:
Prepare using KRAFT 2% Milk Shredded Cheddar Cheese.

VARIATION:
Omit salsa. Prepare as directed, decreasing oven temperature to 375°F, increasing water to 1⅔ cups and adding 1 Tbsp. chili powder with beans and tomato sauce.

TACO BELL® and HOME ORIGINALS® are trademarks owned and licensed by Taco Bell Corp.

STOVE TOP
easy turkey bake

PREP: 10 min. | TOTAL: 40 min. | MAKES: 6 servings.

▶ what you need!

1⅔ cups hot water

1 pkg. (6 oz.) STOVE TOP Stuffing Mix for Turkey

4 cups chopped cooked turkey

1 pkg. (14 oz.) frozen broccoli florets, thawed, drained

1 can (10¾ oz.) condensed cream of chicken soup

¾ cup milk

1½ cups KRAFT Shredded Cheddar Cheese

▶ make it!

HEAT oven to 350°F.

1. **ADD** hot water to stuffing mix; stir just until moistened.

2. **COMBINE** turkey and broccoli in 13×9-inch baking dish. Mix soup, milk and cheese; pour over turkey mixture. Top with stuffing.

3. **BAKE** 30 min. or until heated through.

VARIATION:
Don't have leftover turkey? Prepare recipe as directed, using chopped cooked chicken and STOVE TOP Stuffing Mix for Chicken instead.

three-cheese chicken penne pasta bake

PREP: 20 min. | TOTAL: 43 min. | MAKES: 4 servings.

▸ what you need!

1½ cups multi-grain penne pasta, uncooked

1 pkg. (9 oz.) fresh spinach leaves

1 lb. boneless skinless chicken breasts, cut into bite-size pieces

1 tsp. dried basil leaves

1 jar (14½ oz.) spaghetti sauce

1 can (14½ oz.) diced tomatoes, drained

2 oz. (¼ of 8-oz. pkg.) PHILADELPHIA Neufchâtel Cheese, cubed

1 cup KRAFT 2% Milk Shredded Mozzarella Cheese, divided

2 Tbsp. KRAFT Grated Parmesan Cheese

▸ make it!

HEAT oven to 375°F.

1. **COOK** pasta as directed on package, adding spinach to the boiling water the last minute.

2. **COOK** and stir chicken and basil in large nonstick skillet sprayed with cooking spray on medium-high heat 3 min. Stir in spaghetti sauce and tomatoes; bring to boil. Simmer on low heat 3 min. or until chicken is done. Stir in Neufchâtel.

3. **DRAIN** pasta mixture; return to pan. Stir in chicken mixture and ½ cup mozzarella. Spoon into 2-qt. casserole or 8-inch square baking dish.

4. **BAKE** 20 min.; top with remaining cheeses. Bake 3 min. or until mozzarella is melted.

SERVING SUGGESTION:
Serve with CRYSTAL LIGHT Iced Tea.

Quick & Simple Sides

Easy accompaniments to any meal

easy cheesy potatoes

PREP: 15 min. | TOTAL: 1 hour 10 min. | MAKES: 10 servings, ½ cup each.

▶ what you need!

1 lb. russet potatoes (about 4 medium), cut into ½-inch chunks

½ lb. (8 oz.) VELVEETA Pasteurized Prepared Cheese Product, cut up

½ cup chopped onions

¼ cup KRAFT Real Mayo Mayonnaise

4 slices OSCAR MAYER Bacon, cooked, drained and crumbled (about ¼ cup)

▶ make it!

HEAT oven to 375°F.

1. **COMBINE** all ingredients except bacon in 8-inch square baking dish sprayed with cooking spray; cover with foil.

2. **BAKE** 45 min.

3. **TOP** with bacon; bake, uncovered, 5 to 10 min. or until potatoes are tender.

corn souffle

PREP: 15 min. | TOTAL: 55 min. | MAKES: 16 servings.

▶ what you need!

2 Tbsp. butter

1 pkg. (8 oz.) PHILADELPHIA Cream Cheese, cubed

1 can (15¼ oz.) whole kernel corn, drained

1 can (14.75 oz.) cream-style corn

1 pkg. (8.5 oz.) corn muffin mix

2 eggs, beaten

1 cup KRAFT Shredded Cheddar Cheese

▶ make it!

HEAT oven to 350°F.

1. **MICROWAVE** butter in medium microwaveable bowl on HIGH 30 sec. or until melted. Stir in cream cheese. Microwave 15 sec. or until cream cheese is softened; stir until cream cheese is completely melted and mixture is well blended. Add next 4 ingredients; mix well.

2. **POUR** into 13×9-inch pan sprayed with cooking spray; top with Cheddar.

3. **BAKE** 40 min. or until golden brown. Cool slightly.

SERVING SUGGESTION:
This dish is versatile enough to pair with your favorite barbecued meat, beef stew, chicken soup or even chili.

SUBSTITUTE:
Prepare using PHILADELPHIA Neufchâtel Cheese.

SPECIAL EXTRA:
Add 2 sliced green onions along with the corns, muffin mix and eggs.

MEXICAN-STYLE CORN SOUFFLE:
Prepare as directed, substituting 1 can (11 oz.) whole kernel corn with chopped red and green peppers for the plain whole kernel corn.

creamy vegetable bake

PREP: 20 min. | **TOTAL:** 50 min. | **MAKES:** 10 servings, ¾ cup each.

▶ what you need!

1 pkg. (8 oz.) PHILADELPHIA Cream Cheese, softened

⅓ cup milk

¼ cup KRAFT Grated Parmesan Cheese

1 tsp. dried basil leaves

4 large carrots, diagonally sliced

½ lb. sugar snap peas

½ lb. fresh asparagus, cut into 1-inch lengths

1 large red bell pepper, chopped

1 pkg. (6 oz.) STOVE TOP Stuffing Mix for Chicken

▶ make it!

HEAT oven to 350°F.

1. **MICROWAVE** cream cheese and milk in large microwaveable bowl on HIGH 1 min. or until cream cheese is melted and mixture is blended when stirred. Add Parmesan and basil; stir until blended. Add vegetables; toss to coat.

2. **SPOON** into greased 13×9-inch baking dish. Prepare stuffing as directed on package; spoon over vegetable mixture.

3. **BAKE** 30 min. or until golden brown.

SUBSTITUTE:
Prepare using PHILADELPHIA Neufchâtel Cheese.

HOW TO SELECT SUGAR SNAP PEAS:
Sugar snap peas are a cross between the common English pea and snow peas. Both the pod and the peas inside are edible. Choose pods that are plump, crisp and bright green. Before using, snap off the stem ends, pulling to remove any strings.

easy cheesy scalloped potatoes

PREP: 30 min. | TOTAL: 1 hour 30 min. | MAKES: 15 servings, ¾ cup each.

▶ what you need!

1 pkg. (8 oz.) PHILADELPHIA Cream Cheese, softened

½ cup BREAKSTONE'S or KNUDSEN Sour Cream

1 cup chicken broth

3 lb. red potatoes (about 9), thinly sliced

1 pkg. (6 oz.) OSCAR MAYER Smoked Ham, chopped

1 pkg. (8 oz.) KRAFT Shredded Cheddar Cheese, divided

1 cup frozen peas

▶ make it!

HEAT oven to 350°F.

1. **MIX** cream cheese, sour cream and broth in large bowl until well blended. Add potatoes, ham, 1¾ cups Cheddar and peas; stir gently to evenly coat all ingredients.

2. **SPOON** into 13×9-inch baking dish sprayed with cooking spray; top with remaining Cheddar.

3. **BAKE** 1 hour or until casserole is heated through and potatoes are tender.

SERVING SUGGESTION:
Balance this creamy, indulgent side dish by serving it alongside cooked lean meat or fish and a steamed green vegetable.

PURCHASING POTATOES:
Look for firm, smooth, well-shaped potatoes that are free of wrinkles, cracks and blemishes. Avoid any with green-tinged skins or sprouting "eyes" or buds.

VARIATION:
Substitute OSCAR MAYER Smoked Turkey for the ham and/or 1 cup frozen mixed vegetables for the peas.

crust topped broccoli cheese bake

PREP: 10 min. | TOTAL: 40 min. | MAKES: 14 servings.

▶ what you need!

½ cup (½ of 8-oz. tub) PHILADELPHIA Chive & Onion Cream Cheese Spread

1 can (10¾ oz.) condensed cream of mushroom soup

½ cup water

2 pkg. (16 oz. each) frozen broccoli florets, thawed, drained

1 cup KRAFT Shredded Cheddar Cheese

1 thawed frozen puff pastry sheet (½ of 17.3-oz. pkg.)

1 egg, beaten

▶ make it!

HEAT oven to 400°F.

1. **MIX** cream cheese spread, soup and water in large bowl until well blended. Stir in broccoli and Cheddar. Spoon into 2½- to 3-qt. shallow rectangular or oval baking dish.

2. **ROLL** pastry sheet on lightly floured surface to fit top of baking dish. Cover dish completely with pastry. Press pastry edges against rim of dish to seal. Brush with egg; pierce with knife to vent.

3. **BAKE** 30 min. or until filling is heated through and pastry is puffed and golden brown.

MAKE AHEAD:
Casserole can be assembled in advance. Refrigerate up to 24 hours. When ready to serve, bake (uncovered) as directed.

VARIATION:
Prepare as directed, using PHILADELPHIA Chive & Onion ⅓ Less Fat than Cream Cheese and KRAFT 2% Milk Shredded Cheddar Cheese.

easy risotto with bacon & peas

PREP: 10 min. | TOTAL: 40 min. | MAKES: 6 servings, 1 cup each.

▶ what you need!

6 slices OSCAR MAYER Bacon, cut into 1-inch pieces

1 onion, chopped

1½ cups medium grain rice, uncooked

2 cloves garlic, minced

3 cans (15 oz. each) chicken broth

4 oz. (½ of 8-oz. pkg.) PHILADELPHIA Cream Cheese, cubed

1 cup frozen peas, thawed

2 Tbsp. chopped fresh parsley

2 Tbsp. KRAFT Grated Parmesan Cheese, divided

▶ make it!

1. **COOK** bacon and onions in large skillet on medium-high heat 5 min. or just until bacon is crisp, stirring occasionally.

2. **ADD** rice and garlic; cook 3 min. or until rice is opaque, stirring frequently. Gradually add ½ can broth, cook and stir 3 min. or until broth is completely absorbed. Repeat with remaining broth, adding the cream cheese with the last addition of broth and cooking 5 min. or until the cream cheese is completely melted and mixture is well blended.

3. **STIR** in peas; cook 2 min. or until peas are heated through, stirring occasionally. Remove from heat. Stir in parsley and 1 Tbsp. Parmesan. Serve topped with remaining Parmesan.

SUBSTITUTE:
Prepare using fat-free reduced-sodium chicken broth.

SERVING SUGGESTION:
Serve with hot crusty bread and a mixed green salad topped with your favorite KRAFT Dressing.

garlic mashed potatoes

PREP: 10 min. | TOTAL: 30 min. | MAKES: 8 servings, about ½ cup each.

▶ what you need!

2½ lb. potatoes (about 7), peeled, quartered

4 cloves garlic, minced

1 tub (8 oz.) PHILADELPHIA Cream Cheese Spread

1 Tbsp. butter or margarine

1 tsp. salt

▶ make it!

1. COOK potatoes and garlic in boiling water in large saucepan 20 min. or until potatoes are tender; drain.

2. MASH potatoes until smooth.

3. STIR in remaining ingredients until well blended.

SERVING SUGGESTION:
Add contrast to the potatoes by serving them with a crisp mixed green salad or vegetable, and lean fish, meat or poultry.

FOOD FACTS:
For best results, use russet or red potatoes since they work best for mashing.

SUBSTITUTE:
Prepare using PHILADELPHIA Chive & Onion Cream Cheese Spread.

MAKE IT EASY:
Use mixer to beat potatoes instead of using a hand masher.

zucchini with parmesan sauce

PREP: 10 min. | TOTAL: 17 min. | MAKES: 8 servings.

▶ what you need!

3 zucchini (1 lb.), cut diagonally into ½-inch-thick slices

2 yellow squash, cut diagonally into ½-inch-thick slices

1 red onion, cut into wedges

1 Tbsp. oil

1 tub (8 oz.) PHILADELPHIA Chive & Onion Cream Cheese Spread

⅓ cup fat-free milk

¼ cup KRAFT Grated Parmesan Cheese

¼ tsp. herb and spice blend seasoning

▶ make it!

1. **COOK** and stir vegetables in hot oil in large skillet 5 to 7 min. or until crisp-tender.

2. **MEANWHILE,** place remaining ingredients in small saucepan; cook on low heat until cream cheese spread is completely melted and mixture is well blended and heated through, stirring occasionally.

3. **SERVE** sauce over vegetables.

HEALTHY LIVING:
Save 4 grams of fat per serving by preparing with PHILADELPHIA Chive & Onion ⅓ Less Fat than Cream Cheese.

oat-topped sweet potato crisp

PREP: 20 min. | TOTAL: 1 hour | MAKES: 8 servings.

▸ what you need!

1 pkg. (8 oz.) PHILADELPHIA Cream Cheese, softened

1 can (40 oz.) cut sweet potatoes, drained

¾ cup packed brown sugar, divided

¼ tsp. ground cinnamon

1 Granny Smith apple, chopped

⅔ cup chopped cranberries

½ cup flour

½ cup old-fashioned or quick-cooking oats, uncooked

⅓ cup cold butter or margarine

¼ cup chopped PLANTERS Pecans

▸ make it!

HEAT oven to 350°F.

1. **BEAT** cream cheese, potatoes, ¼ cup sugar and cinnamon with mixer until well blended. Spoon into 1½-qt. casserole; top with apples and cranberries.

2. **MIX** flour, oats and remaining sugar in medium bowl; cut in butter until mixture resembles coarse crumbs. Stir in nuts. Sprinkle over fruit layer in casserole.

3. **BAKE** 35 to 40 min. or until heated through.

SUBSTITUTE:
Prepare using PHILADELPHIA Neufchâtel Cheese.

broccoli & cauliflower supreme

PREP: 25 min. | **TOTAL: 25 min.** | **MAKES: 6 servings.**

▶ what you need!

4 oz. (½ of 8-oz. pkg.) PHILADELPHIA Fat Free Cream Cheese, cubed

¼ cup KRAFT FREE Peppercorn Ranch Dressing

1 Tbsp. GREY POUPON Dijon Mustard

1½ bunches broccoli, cut into florets (about 6 cups), steamed, drained

½ head cauliflower, cut into florets (about 3 cups), steamed, drained

12 RITZ Reduced Fat Crackers, crushed (about ½ cup)

▶ make it!

1. **MICROWAVE** cream cheese, dressing and mustard in medium microwaveable bowl on HIGH 30 to 45 sec. or until cream cheese is softened and sauce is heated through. Stir until cream cheese is completely melted and sauce is well blended.

2. **COMBINE** vegetables in large bowl. Add sauce; toss until vegetables are evenly coated.

3. **TRANSFER** to serving bowl; top with cracker crumbs.

SUBSTITUTE:
Prepare using frozen broccoli and cauliflower florets.

NUTRITION BONUS:
Delight your family with this creamy and delicious, yet low-fat side dish that is high in both vitamins A and C from the broccoli.

cheesy rice & corn casserole

PREP: 10 min. | TOTAL: 35 min. | MAKES: 8 servings, ½ cup each.

▸ what you need!

½ cup (½ of 8-oz. tub) PHILADELPHIA Chive & Onion Cream Cheese Spread

1 egg

2 cups cooked instant white rice

1 can (15¼ oz.) corn with red and green bell peppers, drained

1 cup KRAFT Mexican Style Finely Shredded Four Cheese, divided

2 Tbsp. chopped fresh cilantro

▸ make it!

HEAT oven to 375°F.

1. **MIX** cream cheese spread and egg in large bowl until well blended. Stir in rice, corn, ¾ cup shredded cheese and cilantro.

2. **POUR** into greased 1½-qt. casserole; top with remaining shredded cheese.

3. **BAKE** 20 to 25 min. or until casserole is heated through and cheese is melted.

SPECIAL EXTRA:
Add 1 to 2 tsp. ground cumin for more Mexican flavor.

5-minute cheesy broccoli toss

PREP: 5 min. | TOTAL: 10 min. | MAKES: 4 servings, about ¾ cup each.

▶ what you need!

4 cups frozen broccoli florets

½ tsp. dry mustard

¼ lb. (4 oz.) VELVEETA Pasteurized Prepared Cheese Product, cut into ½-inch cubes

1 Tbsp. KRAFT Grated Parmesan Cheese

▶ make it!

1. **COMBINE** broccoli, mustard and VELVEETA in large nonstick skillet on medium-high heat.

2. **COOK** 5 min. or until broccoli is crisp-tender and mixture is heated through, stirring occasionally.

3. **SPRINKLE** with Parmesan.

SPECIAL EXTRA:
Add 1 minced garlic clove with the broccoli.

bacon-spinach bites

PREP: 10 min. | TOTAL: 30 min. | MAKES: 12 servings.

▶ what you need!

4 oz. (½ of 8-oz. pkg.) PHILADELPHIA Cream Cheese, softened

4 green onions, sliced

1 pkg. (10 oz.) frozen chopped spinach, thawed, squeezed dry

6 slices OSCAR MAYER Bacon, cooked, crumbled

3 Tbsp. flour

4 eggs, beaten

¼ lb. (4 oz.) VELVEETA Pasteurized Prepared Cheese Product, cut into 12 cubes

▶ make it!

HEAT oven to 350°F.

1. **MIX** cream cheese and onions in medium bowl. Add spinach, bacon and flour; mix well. Stir in eggs.

2. **SPOON** into 12 greased and floured muffin pan cups. Top each with 1 VELVEETA cube; press gently into center of filling.

3. **BAKE** 20 min. or until centers are set and tops are golden brown. Serve warm or chilled.

MINIATURE BACON-SPINACH BITES:
Prepare spinach mixture as directed; spoon into 24 greased and floured miniature muffin pan cups. Cut VELVEETA into 24 cubes; press 1 into batter in each cup. Bake 14 to 16 min. or until centers are set and tops are golden brown. Makes 12 servings, 2 bites each.

cheesy chipotle vegetable bake

PREP: 15 min. | TOTAL: 50 min. | MAKES: 10 servings, ¾ cup each.

▸ what you need!

4 cups small cauliflower florets

4 large zucchini, sliced

3 carrots, sliced

2 Tbsp. chopped chipotle peppers in adobo sauce

¼ cup KRAFT Zesty Italian Dressing

½ lb. (8 oz.) VELVEETA Pasteurized Prepared Cheese Product, thinly sliced

20 RITZ Crackers, crushed

2 Tbsp. butter or margarine, melted

▸ make it!

HEAT oven to 375°F.

1. **COMBINE** first 5 ingredients; spoon into 13×9-inch baking dish. Top with VELVEETA.

2. **MIX** cracker crumbs and butter; sprinkle over vegetable mixture.

3. **BAKE** 30 to 35 min. or until vegetables are tender and casserole is heated through.

MAKE AHEAD:
Assemble casserole as directed. Store in refrigerator until ready to bake as directed.

easy cheesy mashed potatoes

PREP: 25 min. | TOTAL: 25 min. | MAKES: 8 servings, about ½ cup each.

▶ what you need!

2 lb. Yukon gold potatoes (about 5), cubed

¼ cup milk

2 oz. VELVEETA Pasteurized Prepared Cheese Product, cut into ½-inch cubes

¼ tsp. garlic powder

1 green onion, thinly sliced

▶ make it!

1. **COOK** potatoes in large saucepan of boiling water 15 min. or until tender. Drain potatoes; return to saucepan.

2. **MASH** potatoes until light and fluffy, gradually adding milk alternately with the VELVEETA.

3. **STIR** in garlic powder. Top with onions.

SPECIAL EXTRA:
For a change of pace, stir ¼ cup OSCAR MAYER Real Bacon Bits into mashed potatoes with garlic powder.

make-ahead broccoli, cheese & rice

PREP: 10 min. | **TOTAL: 20 min.** | **MAKES: 12 servings, ½ cup each.**

▶ what you need!

6 cups fresh broccoli florets

1 can (14½ oz.) fat-free reduced-sodium chicken broth

2 cups instant white rice, uncooked

½ lb. (8 oz.) VELVEETA Pasteurized Prepared Cheese Product, cut into ½-inch cubes

1½ Tbsp. butter

10 RITZ Crackers, crushed

2 Tbsp. KRAFT Grated Parmesan Cheese

▶ make it!

1.

BRING broccoli and broth to boil in medium saucepan on medium-high heat. Stir in rice; cover. Remove from heat. Let stand 5 min. Stir in VELVEETA. Let stand, covered, 5 min. Stir until VELVEETA is completely melted. Spoon into microwaveable bowl; cover with plastic wrap. Refrigerate up to 24 hours.

2.

MEANWHILE, melt butter in small skillet on medium heat. Add cracker crumbs; cook 2 to 3 min. or until golden brown, stirring frequently. Cool completely. Stir in Parmesan; spoon into resealable plastic bag. Seal bag. Store at room temperature up to 24 hours.

3.

COVER broccoli mixture with waxed paper. Microwave on HIGH 5 to 6 min. or until broccoli mixture is heated through; stir. Sprinkle with crumb mixture. Microwave, uncovered, 2 to 3 min. or until heated through.

VARIATION:
Prepare using fat-free reduced-sodium chicken broth and VELVEETA 2% Milk Pasteurized Prepared Cheese Product.

zesty grilled veggies

PREP: 10 min. | **TOTAL:** 20 min. | **MAKES:** 8 servings.

▶ what you need!

4 zucchini (1½ lb.), cut diagonally into ½-inch-thick slices

3 each: red and yellow peppers (1¾ lb.), cut into ½-inch-wide strips

¼ cup KRAFT Zesty Italian Dressing

¼ cup KRAFT Grated Parmesan Cheese

▶ make it!

1. **HEAT** grill to medium heat. Place vegetables in grill basket.

2. **GRILL** 10 min. or until crisp-tender, turning occasionally. Place in large bowl.

3. **ADD** dressing; toss to coat. Sprinkle with cheese.

COOKING KNOW-HOW:
Don't have a grill basket? Cover grill grate with large sheet of heavy-duty foil before heating as directed. Spread vegetables onto foil. Grill as directed, stirring occasionally.

HOW TO BUY PEPPERS:
Look for peppers with very bright colors and a firm thick flesh. Refrigerate unwashed peppers in a plastic bag for up to 2 weeks.

fresh vegetable medley

PREP: 10 min. | TOTAL: 25 min. | MAKES: 12 servings, about ½ cup each.

▸ what you need!

1 small onion, chopped

1 Tbsp. margarine

½ lb. (8 oz.) VELVEETA Pasteurized Prepared Cheese Product, cut into ½-inch cubes

1 can (10¾ oz.) condensed cream of mushroom soup

8 cups mixed fresh vegetables (broccoli and cauliflower florets; sliced carrots, squash and zucchini; cut-up green beans; corn)

▸ make it!

1. **COOK** and stir onions in margarine in large skillet on medium heat until crisp-tender.

2. **ADD** VELVEETA and soup; cook until VELVEETA is completely melted and mixture is well blended, stirring frequently.

3. **STIR** in remaining vegetables; cook 10 min. or until crisp-tender, stirring frequently.

SHORTCUT:
To shave even more time off this easy recipe, purchase cut-up fresh vegetables from the supermarket salad bar. Or, substitute 2 pkg. (16 oz. each) frozen mixed vegetables for the 8 cups mixed fresh vegetables.

VELVEETA classic potatoes au gratin

PREP: 15 min. | TOTAL: 40 min. | MAKES: 8 servings, about ½ cup each.

▶ what you need!

1½ lb. potatoes (about 3 large), thinly sliced

½ lb. (8 oz.) VELVEETA 2% Milk Pasteurized Prepared Cheese Product, cut into ½-inch cubes

½ cup chopped onions

¼ cup milk

1 tsp. dry mustard

½ tsp. black pepper

▶ make it!

HEAT oven to 350°F.

1. **COOK** potatoes in boiling water in large saucepan 8 to 10 min. or just until tender; drain.

2. **TOSS** potatoes with remaining ingredients in 2-qt. casserole; cover with lid.

3. **BAKE** 22 to 25 min. or until potatoes are tender. Stir gently before serving.

SERVING SUGGESTION:
Add contrast to the potatoes by adding a crisp mixed green salad alongside cooked lean fish, meat or poultry.

Showstopping Desserts

Simply stunning desserts

triple-chocolate bliss cake

PREP: 20 min. | TOTAL: 2 hours (incl. cooling) | MAKES: 18 servings.

▶ what you need!

1 pkg. (2-layer size) chocolate cake mix

1 cup BREAKSTONE'S or KNUDSEN Sour Cream

1 pkg. (3.9 oz.) JELL-O Chocolate Instant Pudding

4 eggs

½ cup oil

½ cup water

3 cups thawed COOL WHIP Whipped Topping, divided

1 pkg. (8 squares) BAKER'S Semi-Sweet Chocolate

1½ cups fresh raspberries

▶ make it!

HEAT oven to 350°F.

1. **BEAT** all ingredients except COOL WHIP, chocolate squares and berries in large bowl with mixer on low speed just until moistened. Beat on medium speed 2 min., stopping occasionally to scrape bottom and side of bowl. Pour into greased 12-cup fluted tube pan or 10-inch tube pan.

2. **BAKE** 50 min. to 1 hour or until toothpick inserted near center comes out clean. Cool cake in pan 10 min. Loosen cake from side of pan; invert onto wire rack. Gently remove pan. Cool cake completely. Transfer to plate.

3. **RESERVE** 2 Tbsp. COOL WHIP. Microwave remaining COOL WHIP and chocolate squares in microwaveable bowl on HIGH 1½ to 2 min. or until chocolate is completely melted and mixture is well blended, stirring after each minute. Drizzle over cake. Immediately drop scant teaspoonfuls of the reserved COOL WHIP around top of cake; draw toothpick through middle of each to resemble star. Fill center of cake with berries. Keep refrigerated.

PHILLY brownie cheesecake

PREP: 10 min. | TOTAL: 6 hours (incl. refrigerating) | MAKES: 16 servings.

▶ what you need!

1 pkg. (19 to 21 oz.) brownie mix (13×9-inch pan size)

4 pkg. (8 oz. each) PHILADELPHIA Cream Cheese, softened

1 cup sugar

1 tsp. vanilla

½ cup BREAKSTONE'S or KNUDSEN Sour Cream

3 eggs

2 squares BAKER'S Semi-Sweet Chocolate

▶ make it!

HEAT oven to 325°F.

1. **PREPARE** brownie batter as directed on package; pour into 13×9-inch pan sprayed with cooking spray. Bake 25 min. or until top is shiny and center is almost set.

2. **MEANWHILE,** beat cream cheese, sugar and vanilla in large bowl with mixer until well blended. Add sour cream; mix well. Add eggs, 1 at a time, mixing on low speed after each just until blended. Gently pour over brownie layer in pan. (Filling will come almost to top of pan.)

3. **BAKE** 40 min. or until center is almost set. Run knife or metal spatula around rim of pan to loosen sides; cool. Refrigerate 4 hours.

4. **MELT** chocolate squares as directed on package; drizzle over cheesecake. Refrigerate 15 min. or until chocolate is firm.

SIZE-WISE:
Balance your food choices throughout the day so you can enjoy a serving of this rich-and-indulgent cheesecake with your loved ones.

berry-berry cake

PREP: 25 min. | TOTAL: 2 hours (incl. cooling) | MAKES: 12 servings.

▶ what you need!

⅓ cup PHILADELPHIA ⅓ Less Fat than Cream Cheese

¾ cup sugar, divided

2 egg whites

2 tsp. lemon zest

1 cup plus 2 tsp. flour, divided

½ tsp. baking soda

⅓ cup BREAKSTONE'S FREE or KNUDSEN FREE Fat Free Sour Cream

3 cups mixed fresh blueberries and raspberries, divided

▶ make it!

HEAT oven to 350°F.

1. **BEAT** reduced-fat cream cheese and ½ cup sugar in large bowl with mixer until well blended. Add egg whites and zest; mix well. Mix 1 cup flour and baking soda. Add to cream cheese mixture alternately with sour cream, beating well after each addition. (Do not overmix.)

2. **SPREAD** onto bottom and 1 inch up side of 9-inch springform pan sprayed with cooking spray. Toss 2 cups berries with remaining sugar and flour; spoon over cream cheese mixture in bottom of pan to within ½ inch of edge.

3. **BAKE** 40 to 45 min. or until toothpick inserted in center comes out clean. Run knife around rim of pan to loosen cake; cool before removing rim. Top cake with remaining berries. Keep refrigerated.

PHILADELPHIA 3-STEP
key lime cheesecake

PREP: 10 min. | TOTAL: 3 hours 50 min. | MAKES: 8 servings.

▶ what you need!

2 pkg. (8 oz. each) PHILADELPHIA Cream Cheese, softened

½ cup sugar

1 tsp. lime zest

2 Tbsp. lime juice

½ tsp. vanilla

2 eggs

1 HONEY MAID Graham Pie Crust (6 oz.)

1 cup thawed COOL WHIP Whipped Topping

▶ make it!

HEAT oven to 350°F.

1. **BEAT** first 5 ingredients with mixer until well blended. Add eggs; mix just until blended.

2. **POUR** into crust.

3. **BAKE** 40 min. or until center is almost set. Cool. Refrigerate 3 hours. Top with COOL WHIP just before serving.

SIZE-WISE:
An occasional dessert can be part of a balanced diet, but remember to keep tabs on portions.

SPECIAL EXTRA:
Garnish with lime slices just before serving.

peanut butter cup pie

PREP: 15 min. | **TOTAL: 4 hours 15 min.** | **MAKES: 10 servings.**

▶ what you need!

1 pkg. (8 oz.) PHILADELPHIA Cream Cheese, softened

½ cup plus 1 Tbsp. creamy peanut butter, divided

1 cup cold milk

1 pkg. (3.4 oz.) JELL-O Vanilla Flavor Instant Pudding

2½ cups thawed COOL WHIP Whipped Topping, divided

1 OREO Pie Crust (6 oz.)

3 squares BAKER'S Semi-Sweet Chocolate

▶ make it!

1. **BEAT** cream cheese and ½ cup peanut butter until well blended. Add milk and dry pudding mix; beat 2 min. Whisk in 1 cup COOL WHIP; spoon into crust. Refrigerate until ready to use.

2. **MEANWHILE,** microwave remaining COOL WHIP and chocolate in microwaveable bowl on HIGH 1½ to 2 min. or until chocolate is completely melted and mixture is well blended, stirring after each minute. Cool completely.

3. **SPREAD** chocolate mixture over pudding layer in crust. Microwave remaining peanut butter in small microwaveable bowl 30 sec.; stir. Drizzle over pie. Refrigerate 4 hours or until firm.

HEALTHY LIVING:
Save 60 calories and 6 grams of fat, including 3 grams of saturated fat, per serving by preparing with PHILADELPHIA Neufchâtel Cheese, fat-free milk, JELL-O Vanilla Flavor Fat Free Sugar Free Instant Pudding and COOL WHIP LITE Whipped Topping.

SUBSTITUTE:
Prepare using JELL-O Chocolate Instant Pudding.

PHILADELPHIA new york-style sour cream-topped cheesecake

PREP: 15 min. | TOTAL: 5 hours 5 min. (incl. refrigerating) | MAKES: 16 servings.

▶ what you need!

1½ cups HONEY MAID Graham Cracker Crumbs

¼ cup (½ stick) butter, melted

1¼ cups sugar, divided

4 pkg. (8 oz. each) PHILADELPHIA Cream Cheese, softened

2 tsp. vanilla, divided

1 container (16 oz.) BREAKSTONE'S or KNUDSEN Sour Cream, divided

4 eggs

2 cups fresh strawberries, sliced

▶ make it!

HEAT oven to 325°F.

1. **LINE** 13×9-inch pan with foil, with ends of foil extending over sides. Mix crumbs, butter and 2 Tbsp. sugar; press onto bottom of pan.

2. **BEAT** cream cheese, 1 cup of the remaining sugar and 1 tsp. vanilla in large bowl with mixer until well blended. Add 1 cup sour cream; mix well. Add eggs, 1 at a time, beating on low speed after each just until blended. Pour over crust.

3. **BAKE** 40 min. or until center is almost set. Mix remaining sour cream, sugar and vanilla; carefully spread over cheesecake. Bake 10 min. Cool completely. Refrigerate 4 hours. Use foil handles to lift cheesecake from pan before cutting to serve; top with berries.

HEALTHY LIVING:
Great news! You'll save 80 calories and 9 grams of fat, including 7 grams of saturated fat, per serving by preparing with PHILADELPHIA Neufchâtel Cheese and BREAKSTONE'S Reduced Fat or KNUDSEN Light Sour Cream.

lemon pudding cheesecake

PREP: 15 min. | **TOTAL:** 6 hours (incl. refrigerating) | **MAKES:** 16 servings.

▶ what you need!

40 NILLA Wafers, crushed (about 1½ cups)

¾ cup plus 1 Tbsp. sugar, divided

3 Tbsp. butter or margarine, melted

4 pkg. (8 oz. each) PHILADELPHIA Cream Cheese, softened

2 Tbsp. flour

2 Tbsp. milk

1 cup BREAKSTONE'S or KNUDSEN Sour Cream

2 pkg. (3.4 oz. each) JELL-O Lemon Flavor Instant Pudding

4 eggs

2 squares BAKER'S White Chocolate

1 cup thawed COOL WHIP Strawberry Whipped Topping

▶ make it!

HEAT oven to 325°F.

1. **MIX** wafer crumbs, 1 Tbsp. sugar and butter; press firmly onto bottom of 9-inch springform pan. Bake 10 min.

2. **BEAT** cream cheese, remaining sugar, flour and milk with mixer until well blended. Add sour cream; mix well. Blend in dry pudding mixes. Add eggs, 1 at a time, mixing on low speed after each just until blended.

3. **BAKE** 1 hour 5 min. to 1 hour 15 min. or until center is almost set. Run knife around rim of pan to loosen cake; cool before removing rim. Refrigerate 4 hours. Meanwhile, prepare chocolate curls from white chocolate. Top cheesecake with COOL WHIP and chocolate curls just before serving.

HOW TO MAKE CHOCOLATE CURLS:

Melt chocolate as directed on package. Spread with spatula into very thin layer on baking sheet. Refrigerate 10 min., or until firm but still pliable. To make curls, push a metal spatula firmly along the baking sheet, under the chocolate, so the chocolate curls as it is pushed. (If chocolate is too firm to curl, let stand a few minutes at room temperature; refrigerate again if it becomes too soft.) Use toothpick to carefully place chocolate curls on waxed paper-covered tray. Refrigerate 15 min. or until firm. Use toothpick to arrange curls on dessert.

ultimate turtle cheesecake

PREP: 30 min. | TOTAL: 6 hours 10 min. (incl. refrigerating) | MAKES: 16 servings.

▶ what you need!

2 cups OREO Chocolate Cookie Crumbs

6 Tbsp. butter or margarine, melted

1 pkg. (14 oz.) KRAFT Caramels

½ cup milk

1 cup chopped PLANTERS Pecans

3 pkg. (8 oz. each) PHILADELPHIA Cream Cheese, softened

¾ cup sugar

1 Tbsp. vanilla

3 eggs

2 squares BAKER'S Semi-Sweet Chocolate

▶ make it!

HEAT oven to 325°F.

1. **MIX** crumbs and butter; press onto bottom and 2 inches up side of 9-inch springform pan.

2. **MICROWAVE** caramels and milk in small microwaveable bowl on HIGH 3 min. or until caramels are completely melted, stirring after each minute. Stir in nuts; pour half into crust. Refrigerate 10 min. Refrigerate remaining caramel mixture for later use.

3. **BEAT** cream cheese, sugar and vanilla with mixer until well blended. Add eggs, 1 at a time, mixing on low speed after each just until blended. Pour over caramel layer in crust.

4. **BAKE** 1 hour 5 min. to 1 hour 10 min. or until center is almost set. Run knife around rim of pan to loosen cake; cool before removing rim. Refrigerate 4 hours.

5. **MICROWAVE** reserved caramel mixture 1 min.; stir. Pour over cheesecake. Melt chocolate as directed on package; drizzle over cheesecake.

PHILADELPHIA chocolate-vanilla swirl cheesecake

PREP: 15 min. | TOTAL: 5 hours 25 min. (incl. refrigerating) | MAKES: 16 servings.

▶ what you need!

20 OREO Cookies, crushed (about 2 cups)

3 Tbsp. butter, melted

4 pkg. (8 oz. each) PHILADELPHIA Cream Cheese, softened

1 cup sugar

1 tsp. vanilla

1 cup BREAKSTONE'S or KNUDSEN Sour Cream

4 eggs

6 squares BAKER'S Semi-Sweet Chocolate, melted, cooled

▶ make it!

HEAT oven to 325°F.

1. **LINE** 13×9-inch pan with foil, with ends of foil extending over sides. Mix cookie crumbs and butter; press onto bottom of pan. Bake 10 min.

2. **BEAT** cream cheese, sugar and vanilla in large bowl with mixer until well blended. Add sour cream; mix well. Add eggs, 1 at a time, mixing after each just until blended.

3. **RESERVE** 1 cup batter. Stir chocolate into remaining batter; pour over crust. Top with spoonfuls of reserved plain batter; swirl with knife.

4. **BAKE** 40 min. or until center is almost set. Cool. Refrigerate 4 hours. Use foil handles to lift cheesecake from pan before cutting to serve. Garnish with chocolate curls, if desired.

HOW TO MAKE CHOCOLATE CURLS:
Let additional square(s) of BAKER'S Semi-Sweet Chocolate come to room temperature.
Carefully draw a vegetable peeler at an angle across the chocolate square to make curls.

PHILADELPHIA
new york cheesecake

PREP: 15 min. | TOTAL: 5 hours 25 min. (incl. refrigerating) | MAKES: 16 servings.

▶ what you need!

20 OREO Cookies, finely crushed (about 2 cups)

3 Tbsp. butter or margarine, melted

5 pkg. (8 oz. each) PHILADELPHIA Cream Cheese, softened

1 cup sugar

3 Tbsp. flour

1 Tbsp. vanilla

1 cup BREAKSTONE'S or KNUDSEN Sour Cream

4 eggs

1 can (21 oz.) cherry pie filling

▶ make it!

HEAT oven to 325°F.

1.

LINE 13×9-inch pan with foil, with ends of foil extending over sides. Mix crumbs and butter; press onto bottom of pan.

2.

BEAT cream cheese, sugar, flour and vanilla with mixer until well blended. Add sour cream; mix well. Add eggs, 1 at a time, mixing on low speed after each just until blended. Pour over crust.

3.

BAKE 40 min. or until center is almost set. Cool completely. Refrigerate 4 hours. Use foil handles to lift cheesecake from pan before cutting to serve. Top with pie filling.

turtle pumpkin pie

PREP: 15 min. | TOTAL: 1 hour 15 min. | MAKES: 10 servings.

▶ what you need!

¼ cup plus 2 Tbsp. caramel ice cream topping, divided

1 HONEY MAID Graham Pie Crust (6 oz.)

½ cup plus 2 Tbsp. chopped PLANTERS Pecans, divided

2 pkg. (3.4 oz. each) JELL-O Vanilla Flavor Instant Pudding

1 cup cold milk

1 cup canned pumpkin

1 tsp. ground cinnamon

½ tsp. ground nutmeg

1 tub (8 oz.) COOL WHIP Whipped Topping, thawed, divided

▶ make it!

1. **POUR** ¼ cup caramel topping into crust; sprinkle with ½ cup nuts.

2. **BEAT** pudding mixes, milk, pumpkin and spices with whisk until blended. Stir in 1½ cups COOL WHIP. Spoon into crust.

3. **REFRIGERATE** 1 hour. Top with remaining COOL WHIP, caramel topping and nuts just before serving.

CREATIVE LEFTOVERS:
Need some ideas for how to use the leftover canned pumpkin? Go to www.kraftfoods.com for recipe suggestions, such as Pumpkin Raisin Bars.

best-ever chocolate fudge layer cake

PREP: 10 min. | TOTAL: 1 hour 30 min. (incl. cooling) | MAKES: 18 servings.

▶ what you need!

1 pkg. (8 squares) BAKER'S Semi-Sweet Chocolate, divided

1 pkg. (2-layer size) chocolate cake mix

1 pkg. (3.9 oz.) JELL-O Chocolate Instant Pudding

4 eggs

1 cup BREAKSTONE'S or KNUDSEN Sour Cream

½ cup oil

½ cup water

1 tub (8 oz.) COOL WHIP Whipped Topping (Do not thaw.)

2 Tbsp. PLANTERS Sliced Almonds

▶ make it!

HEAT oven to 350°F.

1. **CHOP** 2 chocolate squares. Beat cake mix, dry pudding mix, eggs, sour cream, oil and water in large bowl with mixer on low speed just until moistened. Beat on medium speed 2 min. Stir in chopped chocolate. Pour into 2 greased 9-inch round pans.

2. **BAKE** 30 to 35 min. or until toothpick inserted in centers comes out clean. Cool in pans on wire racks 10 min. Loosen cakes from sides of pans. Invert onto racks; gently remove pans. Cool cakes completely.

3. **PLACE** COOL WHIP and remaining chocolate squares in microwaveable bowl. Microwave on HIGH 1½ min. or until chocolate is completely melted and mixture

is well blended, stirring after 1 min. Let stand 15 min. to thicken. Stack cake layers on plate, filling and frosting with COOL WHIP mixture. Garnish with nuts. Keep refrigerated.

VARIATION:
Prepare as directed, using JELL-O Chocolate Fat Free Sugar Free Instant Pudding, BREAKSTONE'S Reduced Fat or KNUDSEN Light Sour Cream and COOL WHIP LITE Whipped Topping.

dark molten chocolate cakes

PREP: 15 min. | TOTAL: 30 min. | MAKES: 6 cakes or 12 servings, ½ cake each.

▶ what you need!

1 pkg. (6 squares) BAKER'S Bittersweet Chocolate

10 Tbsp. butter

1½ cups powdered sugar

½ cup flour

3 whole eggs

3 egg yolks

▶ make it!

HEAT oven to 425°F.

1. **GREASE** 6 (6-oz.) custard cups or souffle dishes. Place on baking sheet.

2. **MICROWAVE** chocolate and butter in large microwaveable bowl on MEDIUM (50%) 2 min. or until butter is melted. Stir with whisk until chocolate is completely melted. Add sugar and flour; mix well. Add whole eggs and egg yolks; beat until well blended. Pour into prepared cups.

3. **BAKE** 14 to 15 min. or until cakes are firm around the edges but still soft in the centers. Let stand 1 min. Run small knife around cakes to loosen; carefully unmold onto dessert plates. Cut in half. Serve warm. Garnish as desired.

MAKE AHEAD:
Batter can be made the day before; pour into prepared custard cups. Cover with plastic wrap; refrigerate. When ready to serve, uncover and bake as directed.

starlight mint cake

PREP: 30 min. | TOTAL: 4 hours 10 min. (incl. refrigerating) | MAKES: 16 servings.

▸ what you need!

1 pkg. (2-layer size) white cake mix

1 cup boiling water

1 pkg. (3 oz.) JELL-O Cherry Flavor Gelatin

30 starlight mints, divided

3 squares BAKER'S White Chocolate, melted

2 Tbsp. BREAKSTONE'S or KNUDSEN Sour Cream

2 drops red food coloring

2 cups thawed COOL WHIP Whipped Topping

▸ make it!

HEAT oven to 350°F.

1. **PREPARE** cake batter and bake as directed on package for 2 (9-inch) round cake layers. Cool cakes in pans 15 min. Pierce cakes with large fork at ½-inch intervals. Add boiling water to gelatin mix; stir 2 min. until completely dissolved. Pour over cakes. Refrigerate 3 hours.

2. **RESERVE** 5 mints for later use. Place 13 of the remaining mints, about 4 inches apart, on parchment paper-covered baking sheet. Bake 5 min. or until mints are melted and each spreads out to 1½- to 2-inch circle. Remove from oven; cool completely before removing from parchment paper. Meanwhile, repeat with remaining 12 mints.

3. **BLEND** 5 reserved mints in blender until finely crushed; place in small bowl. Stir in melted chocolate, sour cream and food coloring.

4. **DIP** bottom of 1 cake pan in warm water 10 sec.; unmold onto serving plate. Spread cake with chocolate mixture. Unmold second cake layer; place on first layer. Frost with COOL WHIP. Refrigerate until ready to serve. Decorate with melted mints.

HOW TO BEND CANDY:
To create a curvy effect on each melted candy, use a metal spatula to carefully remove melted candy from parchment while still warm and pliable. Slide candy onto the handle of a wooden spoon or any other object that will bend the candy. Cool completely before using to decorate cake.

raspberry angel cake

PREP: 20 min. | **TOTAL:** 3 hours 20 min. | **MAKES:** 16 servings.

▶ what you need!

3 cups boiling water

2 pkg. (3 oz. each) JELL-O Raspberry Flavor Gelatin

1 pkg. (12 oz.) frozen red raspberries (Do not thaw.)

1 pkg. (7.5 oz.) round angel food cake, cut into 21 thin slices

1 cup thawed COOL WHIP Whipped Topping

▶ make it!

1.

ADD boiling water to gelatin mixes in medium bowl; stir 2 min. until completely dissolved. Add raspberries; stir until thawed. Pour into 9-inch round pan sprayed with cooking spray.

2.

ARRANGE cake slices in concentric circles over gelatin, with slices overlapping as necessary to completely cover gelatin.

3.

REFRIGERATE 3 hours or until gelatin is firm. Unmold onto plate; top with COOL WHIP. Garnish with fresh raspberries and mint, if desired.

HOW TO UNMOLD DESSERT:

Dip knife in warm water and run knife around edge of chilled dessert to loosen. Dip pan in warm water, just to rim, for 15 sec. Lift from water and gently pull gelatin from edge of pan with moistened fingers. Place serving plate on top of pan. Invert pan and plate and shake to loosen dessert. Gently remove pan.

shortcut carrot cake

PREP: 30 min. | TOTAL: 1 hour 30 min. (incl. cooling) | MAKES: 18 servings.

▶ what you need!

1 pkg. (2-layer size) spice cake mix

2 cups shredded carrots (about 3 large)

1 can (8 oz.) crushed pineapple, drained

1 cup chopped PLANTERS Pecans, divided

2 pkg. (8 oz. each) PHILADELPHIA Cream Cheese, softened

2 cups powdered sugar

1 tub (8 oz.) COOL WHIP Whipped Topping, thawed

▶ make it!

HEAT oven to 350°F.

1. **PREPARE** cake batter as directed on package; stir in carrots, pineapple and ¾ cup nuts. Pour into 2 (9-inch) square pans. Bake 25 to 30 min. or until toothpick inserted in centers comes out clean. Cool in pans 10 min.; invert onto wire racks. Remove pans. Turn cakes over; cool completely.

2. **MEANWHILE,** beat cream cheese and sugar until well blended. Whisk in COOL WHIP.

3. **STACK** cake layers on plate, spreading frosting between layers and on top and sides of cake. Top with remaining nuts. Keep refrigerated.

FOR A DECORATIVE DESIGN:
Use a toothpick to draw 4 diagonal lines across top of cake; sprinkle remaining ¼ cup nuts over lines.

chocolate mousse torte

PREP: 20 min. | TOTAL: 3 hours 20 min. | MAKES: 16 servings.

▸ what you need!

37 NILLA Wafers, divided

4 squares BAKER'S Semi-Sweet Chocolate, divided

2 pkg. (3.9 oz. each) JELL-O Chocolate Instant Pudding

2 cups plus 2 Tbsp. cold milk, divided

1 tub (8 oz.) COOL WHIP Whipped Topping, thawed, divided

1 pkg. (8 oz.) PHILADELPHIA Cream Cheese, softened

¼ cup sugar

¾ cup fresh raspberries

▸ make it!

1.  **STAND** 16 wafers around inside edge of 9-inch round pan lined with plastic wrap. Melt 3 chocolate squares as directed on package.

2.  **BEAT** pudding mixes and 2 cups milk with whisk 2 min. Add melted chocolate; mix well. Stir in 1 cup COOL WHIP; pour into prepared pan. Beat cream cheese, sugar and remaining milk with mixer until well blended.

3.  **STIR** in 1 cup of the remaining COOL WHIP; spread over pudding. Top with remaining wafers. Refrigerate 3 hours.

4.  **MEANWHILE**, shave remaining chocolate square into curls. Invert torte onto plate. Remove pan and plastic wrap. Top torte with remaining COOL WHIP, berries and chocolate curls.

snowball cake

PREP: 15 min. | **TOTAL:** 2 hours 20 min. (incl. cooling) | **MAKES:** 16 servings.

▸ what you need!

1 pkg. (2-layer size) devil's food cake mix

1 pkg. (8 oz.) PHILADELPHIA Cream Cheese, softened

1 egg

2 Tbsp. granulated sugar

1 pkg. (3.4 oz.) JELL-O Vanilla Flavor Instant Pudding

¼ cup powdered sugar

1 cup cold milk

1 tub (8 oz.) COOL WHIP Whipped Topping, thawed

1 cup BAKER'S ANGEL FLAKE Coconut

▸ make it!

HEAT oven to 350°F.

1.  **PREPARE** cake batter in 2½-qt. ovenproof bowl, as directed on package; scrape side of bowl. Beat cream cheese, egg and granulated sugar until well blended.

2.  **SPOON** into center of batter in bowl. Bake 1 hour 5 min. or until toothpick inserted in center comes out clean. Cool cake in bowl 10 min.

3.  **LOOSEN** cake from bowl with knife; invert onto wire rack. Remove bowl; cool completely. Beat dry pudding mix, powdered sugar and milk in medium bowl with whisk 2 min.

4.  **STIR** in COOL WHIP. Refrigerate until ready to use. Place cake on plate; frost with pudding mixture. Cover with coconut. Keep refrigerated.

ultimate chocolate caramel pecan pie

PREP: 30 min. | TOTAL: 3 hours 15 min. (incl. refrigerating) | MAKES: 10 servings.

▶ what you need!

3 cups chopped PLANTERS Pecans, divided

¼ cup granulated sugar

¼ cup (½ stick) butter or margarine, melted

1 pkg. (14 oz.) KRAFT Caramels

⅔ cup whipping cream, divided

1 pkg. (8 squares) BAKER'S Semi-Sweet Chocolate

¼ cup powdered sugar

½ tsp. vanilla

▶ make it!

HEAT oven to 350°F.

1. **BLEND** 2 cups nuts in blender until finely ground, using pulsing action. Mix with granulated sugar and butter; press onto bottom and up side of 9-inch pie plate. Bake 12 to 15 min. or until lightly browned. Cool completely. (If crust puffs up during baking, gently press down with back of spoon.)

2. **MICROWAVE** caramels and ⅓ cup whipping cream in microwaveable bowl on HIGH 2½ to 3 min. or until caramels are completely melted and mixture is well blended, stirring after each minute. Pour into crust. Chop remaining nuts; sprinkle over caramel layer.

3. **COOK** chocolate, remaining whipping cream, powdered sugar and vanilla in saucepan on low heat just until chocolate is completely melted, stirring constantly. Pour over pie; gently spread to evenly cover top. Refrigerate 2 hours.

SIZE-WISE:
Serve this decadent pie at your next annual holiday celebration. Follow the serving size and enjoy each bite of this once-a-year treat!

luscious four-layer pumpkin cake

PREP: 20 min. | TOTAL: 1 hour 50 min. (incl. cooling) | MAKES: 16 servings.

▸ what you need!

1 pkg. (2-layer size) yellow cake mix

1 can (15 oz.) pumpkin, divided

½ cup milk

⅓ cup oil

4 eggs

1½ tsp. pumpkin pie spice, divided

1 pkg. (8 oz.) PHILADELPHIA Cream Cheese, softened

1 cup powdered sugar

1 tub (8 oz.) COOL WHIP Whipped Topping, thawed

¼ cup caramel ice cream topping

¼ cup PLANTERS Pecan Halves

▸ make it!

HEAT oven to 350°F.

1. **BEAT** cake mix, 1 cup pumpkin, milk, oil, eggs and 1 tsp. spice in large bowl with mixer until well blended. Pour into 2 greased and floured 9-inch round pans. Bake 28 to 30 min. or until toothpick inserted in centers comes out clean. Cool in pans 10 min. Remove from pans to wire racks; cool completely.

2. **BEAT** cream cheese in medium bowl with mixer until creamy. Add sugar, remaining pumpkin and spice; mix well. Gently stir in COOL WHIP.

3. **CUT** each cake layer horizontally in half with serrated knife; stack on serving plate, spreading cream cheese filling between layers. (Do not frost top layer.) Drizzle with caramel topping just before serving; top with nuts. Refrigerate leftovers.

SIZE-WISE:
Celebrate and enjoy a serving of this indulgent cake on a special occasion.

Oven-Free Classics

No-bake delights everyone will love

double-dipped strawberries

PREP: 10 min. | TOTAL: 10 min. | MAKES: 10 servings, 1 dipped strawberry each.

▶ ## what you need!

10 fresh strawberries (about 1 pt.), washed, well dried

4 squares BAKER'S Semi-Sweet Chocolate, melted

8 OREO Cookies, coarsely crushed (about 1 cup crumbs)

▶ ## make it!

1. **DIP** strawberries in melted chocolate; roll in crumbs.

2. **PLACE** on waxed paper-covered baking sheet; let stand until chocolate is firm.

SUBSTITUTE:
Prepare using BAKER'S Premium White Chocolate.

EASY MICROWAVE MELTING OF BAKER'S CHOCOLATE SQUARES:
Microwave 1 unwrapped square of BAKER'S Chocolate in microwaveable bowl on HIGH 1 min., stirring after 30 sec. or until chocolate is almost melted. (The square will retain its shape.) Stir 1 min. or until chocolate is completely melted. Add 10 sec. for each additional square of chocolate, stirring every 30 sec.

angel lush with pineapple

PREP: 15 min. | TOTAL: 1 hour 15 min. | MAKES: 10 servings.

▶ what you need!

1 can (20 oz.) DOLE Crushed Pineapple in Juice, undrained

1 pkg. (3.4 oz.) JELL-O Vanilla Flavor Instant Pudding

1 cup thawed COOL WHIP Whipped Topping

1 pkg. (10 oz.) round angel food cake, cut into 3 layers

1 cup fresh mixed berries

▶ make it!

1. **MIX** pineapple and dry pudding mix. Gently stir in COOL WHIP.

2. **STACK** cake layers on plate, spreading pudding mixture between layers and on top of cake.

3. **REFRIGERATE** 1 hour. Top with berries.

DOLE is a registered trademark of Dole Food Company, Inc. Kraft Kitchens.

VARIATION:
Prepare using 1 pkg. (1 oz.) JELL-O Vanilla Flavor Fat Free Sugar Free Instant Pudding and COOL WHIP LITE Whipped Topping.

HOW TO CUT CAKE:
Use toothpicks to mark cake into 3 layers. Use a serrated knife to cut cake, in sawing motion, into layers.

LEMON-BERRY LUSH WITH PINEAPPLE:
Prepare using JELL-O Lemon Flavor Instant Pudding.

OREO ice cream shop pie

PREP: 15 min. | TOTAL: 4 hours 15 min. | MAKES: 10 servings.

▶ what you need!

½ cup hot fudge ice cream topping, divided

1 OREO Pie Crust (6 oz.)

1 tub (8 oz.) COOL WHIP Whipped Topping, thawed, divided

2 pkg. (4.2 oz. each) JELL-O OREO Flavor Instant Pudding

1¼ cups cold milk

▶ make it!

1. **RESERVE** 2 Tbsp. fudge topping; spread remaining onto bottom of crust. Cover with half the COOL WHIP. Freeze 10 min.

2. **BEAT** pudding mixes and milk in large bowl with whisk 2 min. (Mixture will be thick.) Stir in remaining COOL WHIP; spoon over COOL WHIP layer in crust.

3. **FREEZE** 4 hours or until firm. Remove pie from freezer 15 min. before serving. Let stand at room temperature to soften slightly. Drizzle with reserved fudge topping.

MAKE IT EASY:
If fudge topping is cold, remove cap and microwave topping on HIGH 30 sec. or until easy to spread.

HOW TO DRIZZLE CHOCOLATE:
Spoon chocolate topping into resealable plastic bag. Use scissors to cut off tiny piece from one bottom corner of bag. Twist top of bag and gently squeeze bag to drizzle chocolate over pie.

tall caramel-banana 'n pecan

PREP: 15 min. | TOTAL: 2 hours 15 min. | MAKES: 8 servings.

▶ what you need!

2 pkg. (8 oz. each) PHILADELPHIA Cream Cheese, softened

½ cup packed brown sugar

1 tsp. vanilla

1 tub (8 oz.) COOL WHIP Whipped Topping, thawed, divided

½ cup caramel ice cream topping, divided

1 HONEY MAID Graham Pie Crust (6 oz.)

½ cup PLANTERS Pecan Pieces

2 bananas, sliced

▶ make it!

1. **BEAT** cream cheese, sugar and vanilla in large bowl with mixer until blended. Stir in 2 cups whipped topping with whisk; set aside.

2. **SPREAD** ¼ cup caramel topping onto bottom of crust; top with layers of ¼ cup pecans, bananas and cream cheese mixture. Cover with remaining whipped topping and pecans.

3. **REFRIGERATE** 2 hours. Drizzle with remaining caramel topping just before serving.

SIZE-WISE:
Sweets can be part of a balanced diet but remember to keep tabs on portions.

SPECIAL EXTRA:
Toast the pecans before using as directed. Garnish with additional PLANTERS Pecan Pieces and additional banana slices just before serving.

frosty orange dream squares

PREP: 20 min. | **TOTAL: 3 hours 20 min.** | **MAKES: 24 servings, 1 square each.**

▶ what you need!

40 NILLA Wafers, finely crushed (about 1½ cups)

¼ cup (½ stick) butter, melted

2 cups cold milk

2 pkg. (4-serving size each) JELL-O Vanilla Flavor Instant Pudding (see note below)

1 tub (8 oz.) COOL WHIP Whipped Topping, thawed, divided

2 cups orange sherbet, softened

▶ make it!

1. **LINE** 13×9-inch pan with foil, with ends of foil extending over sides of pan. Mix wafer crumbs and butter. Press onto bottom of prepared pan; set aside.

2. **ADD** milk to dry pudding mixes in medium bowl. Beat with wire whisk 2 min. or until well blended. Gently stir in half of the whipped topping. Spoon evenly over crust. Refrigerate 10 min. Add remaining whipped topping to sherbet; stir with wire whisk until well blended. Spoon over pudding layer; cover.

3. **FREEZE** at least 3 hours. Use foil handles to remove dessert from pan before cutting into squares to serve. Garnish as desired. Store leftovers in freezer.

NOTE FROM THE KRAFT KITCHENS:
For best texture, do not prepare recipe with JELL-O Fat Free Sugar Free Instant Pudding.

FROSTY ORANGE DREAM PIE:
Prepare as directed, substituting 1 HONEY MAID Graham Pie Crust (6 oz.) for the homemade crust and cutting all remaining ingredients in half.

SUBSTITUTE:
Prepare as directed, using lemon or lime sherbet and/or COOL WHIP LITE Whipped Topping.

chocolate frozen OREO bash

PREP: 15 min. | TOTAL: 3 hours 15 min. | MAKES: 16 servings.

▶ what you need!

16 OREO Cookies

2 squares BAKER'S Semi-Sweet Chocolate, divided

1 pkg. (8 oz.) PHILADELPHIA Cream Cheese, softened

⅓ cup sugar

1 tub (6 oz.) COOL WHIP Chocolate Whipped Topping, thawed

¼ cup milk

▶ make it!

1. **ARRANGE** cookies in single layer on bottom of 8- or 9-inch square pan. Melt chocolate squares as directed on package; set aside.

2. **BEAT** cream cheese and sugar in large bowl with electric mixer on medium speed until well blended. Add chocolate; beat until well blended. Gently stir in whipped topping. Blend in milk. Pour over cookie layer in pan.

3. **FREEZE** several hours or until firm. Remove from freezer about 15 min. before serving; let stand in refrigerator until dessert can easily be cut. Store leftover dessert in freezer.

SUBSTITUTE:
Prepare as directed, using regular COOL WHIP Whipped Topping.

JAZZ IT UP:
Garnish with fresh raspberries, if desired.

"no-pan" ice cream sandwich dessert

PREP: 15 min. | TOTAL: 4 hours 15 min. | MAKES: 12 servings, 1 slice each.

▶ what you need!

1 cup fresh raspberries, divided

1 cup sliced fresh strawberries, divided

1 tub (8 oz.) COOL WHIP Whipped Topping, thawed, divided

12 rectangular vanilla ice cream sandwiches

▶ make it!

1. **PLACE** ½ cup each raspberries and strawberries in medium bowl. Mash lightly with fork. Gently stir in 1½ cups of the whipped topping.

2. **ARRANGE** 4 of the ice cream sandwiches, side-by-side, on 24-inch-long piece of foil; spread with half of the whipped topping mixture. Repeat layers. Top with remaining 4 ice cream sandwiches. Frost top and sides with remaining whipped topping. Bring up foil sides. Double fold top and ends to loosely seal packet.

3. **FREEZE** at least 4 hours before slicing to serve. Store leftovers in freezer.

   JAZZ IT UP:
   Prepare as directed, using Neapolitan ice cream sandwiches.

sweet peanut brittle

PREP: 5 min. | TOTAL: 50 min. | MAKES: About 1½ lb. or 16 servings.

▶ what you need!

1 cup sugar

½ cup light corn syrup

1 Tbsp. butter

2 cups PLANTERS COCKTAIL Peanuts

1 tsp. baking soda

1 tsp. vanilla

4 squares BAKER'S Semi-Sweet Chocolate

¼ cup creamy peanut butter

▶ make it!

1. **SPRAY** large baking sheet with cooking spray. Microwave sugar and corn syrup in large glass microwaveable bowl on HIGH 5 min. Stir in butter and peanuts. Microwave 3 to 4 min. or until pale golden brown. Stir in baking soda and vanilla. (Mixture will foam.) Spread onto prepared baking sheet. Cool completely. Break into pieces.

2. **MICROWAVE** chocolate in 1-cup glass measuring cup on HIGH 1 to 2 min. or until chocolate is melted when stirred. Add peanut butter; stir until melted. Dip half of each candy piece in chocolate mixture; scrape bottom against edge of cup to remove excess chocolate. Place on sheet of foil or waxed paper. Refrigerate 20 min. or until chocolate is firm.

SIZE-WISE:
Trying to pace your eating at a party? Preview your choices and be selective instead of taking some of everything.

CAUTION:
Use heavy oven mitts or potholders when removing bowl from microwave as candy mixture will be extremely hot. If available, use a 2-qt. glass measuring cup with handle as a large microwaveable bowl.

HOT/SWEET PEANUT BRITTLE:
Stir 1 tsp. hot pepper sauce into candy along with the vanilla.

NILLA-chocolate tiramisu cups

PREP: 30 min. | **TOTAL: 4 hours 30 min. (incl. refrigerating)** | **MAKES: 12 servings.**

▸ what you need!

4 squares BAKER'S Semi-Sweet Chocolate

1 Tbsp. butter or margarine

24 NILLA Wafers, divided

1 Tbsp. MAXWELL HOUSE Instant Coffee

2 Tbsp. hot water

1 pkg. (8 oz.) PHILADELPHIA Cream Cheese, softened

¼ cup sugar

1 tub (8 oz.) COOL WHIP Whipped Topping, thawed

6 fresh strawberries, halved

▸ make it!

1. **MICROWAVE** chocolate and butter in microwaveable bowl on HIGH 1½ min., stirring after 1 min. Stir until chocolate is completely melted. Spoon into 12 foil cup-lined muffin cups; brush chocolate onto bottom and halfway up side of each cup. Place 1 wafer in each cup. Refrigerate until ready to use.

2. **DISSOLVE** coffee in hot water. Place cream cheese and sugar in medium bowl. Gradually add coffee mixture, beating with whisk after each addition. Stir in whipped topping. Spoon ½ the cream cheese mixture into cups; top with remaining wafers and cream cheese mixture.

3. **REFRIGERATE** 4 hours or until set. Top with strawberries.

SPECIAL EXTRA:
Top each cup with an additional NILLA Wafer just before serving.

MAKE AHEAD:
Chocolate cups can be prepared ahead and stored, unfilled, in refrigerator up to 2 days.

OREO cookie cream pie

PREP: 30 min. | TOTAL: 4 hours 30 min. (incl. refrigerating) | MAKES: 10 servings.

▶ what you need!

24 OREO Chocolate Sandwich Cookies, divided

2 Tbsp. butter or margarine, melted

2 cups cold milk

2 pkg. (3.4 oz. each) JELL-O White Chocolate Flavor Instant Pudding & Pie Filling

2 cups thawed COOL WHIP Whipped Topping

½ cup fresh raspberries

½ square BAKER'S Semi-Sweet Chocolate, shaved into curls

▶ make it!

1. **CRUSH** 16 cookies. Mix with butter; press onto bottom and up side of 9-inch pie plate. Chop 8 remaining cookies; set aside.

2. **BEAT** milk and pudding mixes with whisk 2 min. Stir in whipped topping and chopped cookies. Spoon into crust. Refrigerate 4 hours.

3. **TOP** with raspberries and chocolate curls just before serving.

HOW TO MAKE CHOCOLATE CURLS:
Warm a square of BAKER'S Chocolate by microwaving it, unwrapped, on HIGH for a few seconds or just until you can smudge the chocolate with your thumb. Hold the square steadily and draw a peeler slowly over flat bottom of square, allowing a thin layer of chocolate to curl as it is peeled off the bottom of the square to make long, delicate curls. Use the same technique along the narrow side of the square to make short curls.

NILLA peppermint cremes

PREP: 30 min. | TOTAL: 3 hours 30 min. (incl. refrigerating) | MAKES: 10 servings, 2 sandwiches each.

▶ what you need!

4 squares BAKER'S Premium White Chocolate

2 Tbsp. whipping cream

1½ tsp. butter or margarine

6 drops peppermint extract

40 NILLA Wafers

4 starlight mints, crushed

▶ make it!

1. **MICROWAVE** chocolate, cream and butter in microwaveable bowl on HIGH 1 to 1½ min. or until butter is melted, stirring after 1 min. Stir until chocolate is completely melted. Blend in extract.

2. **REFRIGERATE** 3 hours or until firm.

3. **SHAPE** 1 tsp. of the chocolate mixture into ½-inch ball; place between 2 wafers to form sandwich. Press together gently. Roll edge in crushed candies; place on waxed paper-covered baking sheet. Repeat to make 20 cookie sandwiches.

HOW TO DOUBLE RECIPE:
This recipe can be easily doubled to make enough for a party. Just prepare as directed, doubling the chocolate, cream, butter, wafers and mints, and using ⅛ tsp. extract.

HOW TO STORE PEPPERMINT CREMES:
Store in tightly covered container in refrigerator up to 2 days.

CHIPS AHOY! warm s'mores

PREP: 5 min. | TOTAL: 6 min. | MAKES: 8 servings.

▶ what you need!

16 CHIPS AHOY! Cookies, divided

2 squares BAKER'S Semi-Sweet Chocolate, chopped

2 tsp. BAKER'S ANGEL FLAKE Coconut

16 JET-PUFFED Miniature Marshmallows

▶ make it!

1. **PLACE** 8 cookies, flat-sides up, on microwaveable plate; top with remaining ingredients.

2. **MICROWAVE** on HIGH 30 sec. or until chocolate is almost melted. Cover with remaining cookies; press down lightly to secure. Microwave 30 sec. or until cookies are warmed and chocolate and marshmallows are melted.

3. **SERVE** warm. Or, cover and refrigerate 5 to 10 min. or until filling is set.

MAKE IT A PARTY!:
Place all ingredients in separate small bowls. If desired, add other filling choices, such as small candies and/or crushed OREO Cookies. Let the kids mix and match the filling ingredients as desired to create their own stuffed cookies!

USE YOUR OVEN:
Heat oven to 350°F. Top 8 cookies as directed; place on foil-covered baking sheet. Bake 4 min. Cover with remaining cookies; press down lightly to secure. Bake 2 to 4 min. or until cookies are warmed and chocolate and marshmallows are melted.

index

chicken & poultry

chocolate

fish & seafood

G

H

L

M

N

O

P

METRIC CONVERSION CHART

VOLUME MEASUREMENTS (dry)

1/8 teaspoon = 0.5 mL
1/4 teaspoon = 1 mL
1/2 teaspoon = 2 mL
3/4 teaspoon = 4 mL
1 teaspoon = 5 mL
1 tablespoon = 15 mL
2 tablespoons = 30 mL
1/4 cup = 60 mL
1/3 cup = 75 mL
1/2 cup = 125 mL
2/3 cup = 150 mL
3/4 cup = 175 mL
1 cup = 250 mL
2 cups = 1 pint = 500 mL
3 cups = 750 mL
4 cups = 1 quart = 1 L

VOLUME MEASUREMENTS (fluid)

1 fluid ounce (2 tablespoons) = 30 mL
4 fluid ounces (1/2 cup) = 125 mL
8 fluid ounces (1 cup) = 250 mL
12 fluid ounces (1 1/2 cups) = 375 mL
16 fluid ounces (2 cups) = 500 mL

WEIGHTS (mass)

1/2 ounce = 15 g
1 ounce = 30 g
3 ounces = 90 g
4 ounces = 120 g
8 ounces = 225 g
10 ounces = 285 g
12 ounces = 360 g
16 ounces = 1 pound = 450 g

DIMENSIONS

1/16 inch = 2 mm
1/8 inch = 3 mm
1/4 inch = 6 mm
1/2 inch = 1.5 cm
3/4 inch = 2 cm
1 inch = 2.5 cm

OVEN TEMPERATURES

250°F = 120°C
275°F = 140°C
300°F = 150°C
325°F = 160°C
350°F = 180°C
375°F = 190°C
400°F = 200°C
425°F = 220°C
450°F = 230°C

BAKING PAN SIZES

Utensil	Size in Inches/Quarts	Metric Volume	Size in Centimeters
Baking or Cake Pan (square or rectangular)	8×8×2	2 L	20×20×5
	9×9×2	2.5 L	23×23×5
	12×8×2	3 L	30×20×5
	13×9×2	3.5 L	33×23×5
Loaf Pan	8×4×3	1.5 L	20×10×7
	9×5×3	2 L	23×13×7
Round Layer Cake Pan	8×1½	1.2 L	20×4
	9×1½	1.5 L	23×4
Pie Plate	8×1¼	750 mL	20×3
	9×1¼	1 L	23×3
Baking Dish or Casserole	1 quart	1 L	—
	1½ quarts	1.5 L	—
	2 quarts	2 L	—